JAKE BUGG

THE BIOGRAPHY

David Nolan

JOHN BLAKE

Published by John Blake Publishing Ltd,
3 Bramber Court, 2 Bramber Road,
London W14 9PB, England

www.johnblakepublishing.co.uk

www.facebook.com/Johnblakepub facebook
twitter.com/johnblakepub twitter

This edition published in 2014

ISBN: 978-1-78219-725-6

British Library Cataloguing-in-Publication Data:

A catalogue record for this book is available from the British Library.

Design by www.envydesign.co.uk

Printed and bound in Great Britain by CPI Group (UK) Ltd

3 5 7 9 10 8 6 4 2

Papers used by John Blake Publishing are natural, recyclable products made
from wood grown in sustainable forests. The manufacturing processes conform
to the environmental regulations of the country of origin.

Every attempt has been made to contact the relevant copyright-holders, but some
were unobtainable. We would be grateful if the appropriate people could contact us.

JAKE BUGG

THE BIOGRAPHY

For Judith – the big sister's big sister.

David Nolan has written books on artists from Emeli Sandé to the Sex Pistols. He's worked on newspapers, magazines and radio and is also an award-winning television-documentary maker.

ACKNOWLEDGEMENTS

The good people of Nottingham – and particularly those involved in the city's music scene – have been very kind to me while writing this book. Many thanks to the following people for their time and help: George Akins, Mike Atkinson, Mark Del, Dean Jackson, Zoe Kirk, Nick McDonald, Gaz Peacham, Dick Stone, Rob Upton, Simon Wilson and everyone at the *Nottingham Post*, and Philip Wright. In each chapter, there's a selection of songs that can act as a soundtrack – put them into the music-providing system of your choice and listen as you read.

CONTENTS

INTRODUCTION

GLASTONBURY

Soundtrack:
Lonnie Donegan – 'Rock Island Line' 1956

It's July 2013 and, although it doesn't know it yet, Britain is on the edge of a heatwave the like of which some people will compare to the summer of 1976. Typical that – people harking back to the old days when everything was better. The music was better, the grass was greener, even the summers were hotter.

Festival season is just getting underway and the daddy of them all is already well into its first day. This year, the line-up for the Glastonbury Festival has something for everyone: the 'not-that-arsed' swagger of Liam Gallagher and Beady Eye, the rockabilly lyricism of Arctic Monkeys, the timeless outlaw stylings of The Rolling Stones, the folky earnestness of

Mumford & Sons, the youthful blues plundering of The Strypes and the cooler-than-thou indie jangle of Johnny Marr.

The festival also has one act that has a little pinch of all the above rolled into one petite, flat-vowelled package. He strolls onto the Pyramid stage as if he's playing an open-mic session at a Nottingham café – something he was doing on a regular basis until recently.

He's been here before and had previously made a genuine attempt to soak up the Glastonbury vibe by camping out. He lasted a night and vowed never to go near a tent again. His view on the festival experience that year was a typically blunt one: 'It's muddy and fucking horrible!' he told journalists backstage. 'I didn't get a hundred-per cent "involved" in the Glasto experience. But it's great to be part of it.'

He is – depending on whose opinion you care to canvass – 'The Council Estate Bob Dylan', 'The Cockiest Lonnie Donegan Wannabe in Nottingham' or 'The King of the Clifton Delta'. Or all three.

He said he wanted to get to Number One and get rid of all the 'Simon Cowell shit'. He did indeed get to the top of the charts and beat Cowell's discovery Leona Lewis along the way.

He's either psychic or very, very sure of his abilities. He's robbed the charts of its pop dominance like Nottingham's very own Robin Hoodie.

Jake Bugg's success has shocked the music industry, annoyed a whole host of boy bands and put the city of Nottingham back on a musical map that it fell off 40 years ago. It's come as quickly and as dramatically as the lightning bolt that he has famously sung about. Add to that the fact that Bugg is barely out of his teens and it begs the question: how did it all happen?

The answer to that can be found just off the Clifton Boulevard in Nottingham...

CHAPTER ONE

THE CLIFTON BOULEVARD

Soundtrack:
Johnny Cash – 'So Doggone Lonesome' 1955
Buddy Holly – 'Blue Days, Black Nights' 1956
The Jimi Hendrix Experience – 'Up From The Skies' 1967

It's always a good idea to mind the gap between your expectation and the reality – none more so when it comes to the swankily titled Clifton Boulevard. It's not, I'm here to report, as glamorous as it sounds. It's a grey slice of flyover/bypass that crosses the River Trent and skirts the south of Nottingham city centre as it takes you to the housing estate of Clifton. The Boulevard – or the A52 Trunk Road if you prefer – will also swing you close to Clifton Village, a slightly more upmarket proposition. But our business lies on the Clifton estate.

Here you'll find row upon row of grey or yellow houses with very little to distinguish one from the other. Occasionally, a little neighbourly one-upmanship can be spotted to break up the monotony: a pebble-dashed house here, a touch of stone cladding there, maybe even a fancy porch or a little fake wooden exterior. It's as if those residents are saying: we're just that little cut above our neighbours and we'd like you and them to know it. They'd still have a long way to go to match the wealth of the neighbouring village of Ruddington. Here the houses are detached, the gates are electric and there is a reassuring gravelly crunch to the driveways.

On the Clifton estate, though, there are signs that the area is changing: the market traders have been shifted temporarily to make way for the new tramline that will connect Clifton with Nottingham city centre. Go past Clifton Football Club and you'll see The Fairham pub and The Peacock – 'Meet and Eat' – as well as the Quality Fish Bar, a new-ish police station, a leisure centre and Clifton Central Park.

Clifton is where Jacob Edwin Kennedy – otherwise known as Jake Bugg – grew up and it's been painted as something of a badlands by those who've written about the young singer in the past. 'It's a good line, isn't it? "Kid from council estate makes good,"' Simon Wilson of the *Nottingham Post* told me. 'But there are worse places in Nottingham... St Anne's, for example. Nottingham briefly had a reputation for guns and gangs. For a while, Nottingham took over from Manchester – we became "Shottingham" and took over from

"Gunchester" to become the gun capital. It was more areas like St Anne's and Meadows, that's where the reputation grew from. So Clifton is just a working-class estate. I think it was the largest council-house estate in Europe when it was built. There are worse places.'

'It's been massively exaggerated, I think,' Jake told journalist Simon Parkin in 2013 when asked about Clifton's tough reputation. 'It was no picnic but it's not as bad as some people would have you believe. It's not easy living on a council estate, it has its bad points as well as good.'

'People from Clifton are almost apologetic that they're from Clifton,' says Rob Upton, DJ at Nottingham's most famous venue, Rock City. 'It's not the worst place in Nottingham by a long stretch but it's not the nicest either. You wouldn't want to live there. It's kind of the wrong side of the ring road.'

Jake was born on 28 February 1994 – he shares the same birthday as Ian Brown of The Stone Roses, a band he'd later tour with. Brown shares something else with Bugg – a similar, moochy, 'not bothered either way, mate' swagger. Jake was named after Jake LaMotta, the Bronx-born boxer immortalised in the Robert De Niro film *Raging Bull*. Twenty years later, Jake would share a sofa with De Niro when the two were guests on *The Graham Norton Show*. 'He was born at Nottingham City Hospital,' Jake's mum Leeysa Kennedy recalled in an interview with the *Nottingham Post*, a newspaper that would spend a great deal of time charting the progress of Jake Bugg. 'I was living in a one-bedroom flat in Clifton at the time and I remember the day I brought him home. I'll never forget it. I often think about those days.'

At the time, Leeysa was married to local lad David Bugg – who still lives in Clifton and works in a nursing home – and both loved and performed music. They even formed a duo; publicity shots of the pair show them looking pouty and moody in an 1980s sort of way. The music was lush, romantic and keyboard heavy, with songs like 'Crying' and 'End of the World'. 'We used to write and perform as a duo called Heaven's Blue. It was the sort of music that Jake would hate: eighties synth pop,' David Bugg later told the *This Is Nottingham* website. 'We carried on when Jake was born and I remember being in a recording studio when he was about three years old and he couldn't keep his hands off the mixing desk. We had to get a taxi to his aunt's to look after him so we could finish the recording.'

The 1980s synth duo made it into the next decade and in 1990 the couple were confident enough to send a demo of their songs to a new radio show that had just started up on their local radio station: *The Beat* hosted by Dean Jackson. 'They were on the programme in its first year,' Jackson told me. 'They were one of the many, many local bands we've had on. Any good? I'm ashamed to say I can't remember. I think it was a synth pop, Thompson Twins kind of thing. It must have been more than passable otherwise we wouldn't have played it.'

Some 20 years later, Jake would follow in the family

tradition and also send a demo into *The Beat*, just like his mum and dad did. It would prove to be one of the key turning points in his career: 'I know that Jake has a copy of the Blue Heaven performance on cassette,' says Dean Jackson. 'It was that performance that first made him think of getting in touch with me.'

David Bugg: 'Me and his mum going on *The Beat* was one of the reasons Jake decided to get in touch with Dean, which obviously led to him being on *BBC Introducing* at Glastonbury and everything that followed. My mum, who was a care worker, used to sing and my dad, a retired heating engineer, played guitar, as do my brothers William and George and my nephew Scott.'

'Jake's granddad Charles was a folk fan and played acoustic guitar,' mum Leeysa later said, describing the musical roots of her side of the family tree. 'He was very much into his folk music and would spend hours playing Donovan and Dylan songs to us kids, keeping us entertained while my mum was pottering around in the kitchen, making our dinner.' Dylan would become a recurring theme in Bugg's career, largely thanks to comparisons made by journalists between Jake's reedy voice and that of the hugely influential American singer. For Jake, though, the comparison has always been a slightly misleading one – a greater influence, he says, was Dylan's British equivalent, Donovan. 'My mum always played [Donovan's] "Catch the Wind",' Jake later said. 'Some of the songs he wrote are just phenomenal – so gorgeous; just really mellow and nice to listen to. People have been comparing me to Bob Dylan too. And he is amazing, don't get me wrong, but maybe a lot of people say that because they don't really know Donovan.'

Dylan's name would be used as a point of comparison with Jake over and over again – perhaps because 'COUNCIL ESTATE BOB DYLAN' makes a better headline than 'COUNCIL ESTATE DONOVAN'. Bugg would insist that his knowledge of Dylan was fleeting: 'I only really like *The Times They Are a-Changin'* album – it's great. I remember when I first listened to it I didn't get it at all. Same with Johnny Cash, Ray Charles. It just something that grows on you.'

The Beatles were regularly played – so were The Rolling Stones – but there was classical music too and even a smattering of Take That. The first album that Bugg recalls listening to was by 1950s rock pioneer Buddy Holly. The bespectacled singer, songwriter and producer created a stripped-down format for playing rock music – vocals, guitar, bass and drums – that's still being followed today, not least by Jake Bugg. Before his tragic death in an air crash in 1959, Holly also single-handedly created the concept that a rock musician could also be a songwriter as well as a performer. Just to rub it in, Holly was also a producer. His jangly, short yet heartfelt songs are still influencing musicians today – and it's there for all to see and hear in the music of Jake Bugg. 'I think it might have been a horrible "Best Of" or something,' Jake later told the *NME* when asked about the first Buddy Holly album he ever owned. 'My nana was a big fan. She says she used to iron his shirts for him. He came to England once and she was working in the theatre he was playing at and she ironed his clothes. I don't know how true that is but she swears it is. I could be sat here with a big pair of specs!'

Another key musical influence would come from an even more unusual source than Jake's gran: *The Simpsons*. The 12-year-old was watching an episode of the long-running cartoon show called *Scuse Me While I Miss The Sky*, which features a meteor shower. The song that plays during the scene is 'Vincent' by American singer-songwriter Don McLean. McLean is probably best known for his song 'American Pie' and his influence on Bugg has a certain symmetry because 'American Pie' tells the story of the night that Buddy Holly was killed in the air crash that also claimed the lives of Latino rocker Richie Valens and DJ and singer The Big Bopper. 'Vincent' – often referred to as 'Starry, Starry Night' after the opening lines – had been a Number One hit in the UK in 1972 and its use on *The Simpsons* seems to have had a profound effect on the young Jake: 'It was the first time I'd actually really liked a piece of music,' he said. 'It definitely led me to go and discover more stuff.'

As well as finding out more about McLean – and realising that the rest of the American singer's material didn't quite strike him in the same way – he made another realisation: 'I remember thinking,' he later told *The Guardian*, 'I want to write songs like that.' Jake would later get the chance to meet McLean, backstage at a gig in Sheffield. The youngster queued up for an autograph, hoping to ask McLean some questions, but in the end he was too shy to speak. McLean had a few words for young Jake though – a little advice: stay in school. 'It was funny, man,' he later recalled in *Q* magazine. 'And no, I didn't stay in school. But I did alright.'

Simon Wilson of the *Nottingham Post*: 'His mum and dad aren't together anymore; they split up when he was quite young. She's just a normal working-class mum really. His dad lives around the corner, still in Clifton. He used to pop round for tea and all the rest of it. He [Jake] was raised by his mum basically but his dad was around, not far away.'

When the couple split up, money was tight for Leeysa – especially after Jake's half-sister Hannah arrived. Jake would often speak about having 'one pair of jeans and one pair of trainers' when he was a kid. Holidays were spent at her parents' bed-and-breakfast at Mablethorpe, a seaside resort in Lincolnshire. With no money for holidays abroad, young Jake would be put on a train and spend breaks from school with his grandparents. It wasn't until Jake's career took off in 2012 that he actually went abroad for the first time and had to get himself a passport.

Back in Clifton, Jake and his friends – all tracksuits and a bit of attitude – would hang around the local precinct. They'd buy a sausage 'cob' – Notts speak for a bread roll – and loiter outside the chip shop. The owner got so fed up he installed a sonic deterrent to try to shift Jake and his mates: this was an electronic device that emitted a high-pitched noise that can only be heard by youngsters. 'I didn't go around causing trouble,' Jake later told the

London Evening Standard. 'I just used to hang around the shops smoking fags. If there was anyone causing trouble I usually knew them, but I just kept my head down and they left me alone.'

Outside of the precinct, life in Clifton for Jake revolved largely around football, football and more football. 'Prior to picking up the guitar he didn't really listen to that much music,' mum Leeysa later explained to Radio 1. 'It was mainly a football focus.'

It's a football town, with Nottingham Forest's presence looming large over the city since the club was founded in 1898 – especially during the years the club was managed by one of football's most colourful and outspoken characters, the late Brian Clough. There were even plans to move the club's ground to Bugg's manor in Clifton at one stage. But despite Forest's fame, it's Notts County that can boast the title of the world's oldest professional football club and that's where Bugg's footballing loyalties lie. They're known as The Magpies because of their black-and-white strip. Bugg, as some of his detractors have pointed out, is something of a magpie too.

As his interest in football grew, Jake's bedroom began to fill with cups and medals – man-of-the-match medals, top goal scorer, awards for good sportsmanship: 'Before I was 12 I didn't have any interest in music at all,' he later said. 'It was all about football. I was playing for four teams at one point. And I played for Nottingham City Boys – but when I picked up a guitar I lost interest for some reason. I'd sit in my bed-room and play the guitar for hours.'

Those dreams of a footballing future were curtailed thanks to that guitar he picked up (later broken thanks to a tumble down the stairs), which for many years sat in Bugg's old bedroom at his mum's house. It was given to him by his uncle, who helped him eke out his first chords. The first song he was taught was 'Mad World', written by Tears For Fears: 'Four chords – G, E minor, D and A... "Mad World". It wasn't the Tears For Fears version I learned.' The version Jake knew was the cover by Gary Jules, which was a Christmas Number One in 2003. He also learned the riff to 'Paranoid' by Black Sabbath and got a song book to learn tunes by American band Green Day. 'That really helped when I was learning the guitar,' he later told DJ Zane Lowe. 'I didn't really know much about chords so I'd look at it and get the shapes together. That really helped. I don't really have a clue what the notes mean. It baffles me.'

'It was his uncle Mark who gave him a guitar,' dad David Bugg later said. 'By which time me and his mum had split up. I didn't know he'd been learning to play it until he came round my house and asked if I'd record him. I had a small studio at home and I remember he did three covers. One of them was Don McLean's "Vincent". Now this was before his voice had broken but when he started singing I could feel the hairs on the back of my neck stand up. And it made me cry. It's one of my favourite songs anyway and I had no idea he had such a talent; a talent he'd not revealed to me until that moment.'

As music began to take over, the football posters on Jake's bedroom wall began to be replaced by the likes of Jimi

Hendrix – the legendary guitarist whose line 'Scuse me while I kiss the sky' from the song 'Purple Haze' had inspired the title of the *Simpsons's* episode that had such an impact – more symmetry: 'Well, when I first heard Jimi Hendrix I thought he was brilliant,' he later told the *Contact Music* website. 'These came around the time I put down the football. But people like Johnny Cash and Dylan, the first time I heard them I didn't really think anything of them at first and that's just something that's grown on me. The Beatles are probably my favourite band in my eyes; I always liked those even when I didn't have an interest in music. A bit of everything really. The old blues stuff from Charlie Patton and Robert Johnson, even a bit of Beethoven, a bit of Mozart is brilliant. It's all good. From that to Oasis or The Arctic Monkeys, whatever sounds good, man.'

To add to classic 1960s guitar bands, Britpop and the blues, an increasingly eclectic mix of music began to form around the teenager: the blissed-out echo guitar of John Martyn's 1973 album *Solid Air*, the downbeat English melancholia of the late Nick Drake's *Pink Moon* from 1972 and, released in the same year, *American Pie* by Don McLean, the album that contained the song 'Vincent'. Jake's bedroom became the place where his musical influences began to gel. 'I'd be lying there singing along to The Beatles and Johnny Cash – that's how I taught myself to sing,' he later told Radio 1. 'Not that I'm a great singer by any means. I think it's about songs. You don't need the best voice – Neil Young and Bob Dylan are examples of that. Loads of people can sing but some people sing with more honesty and from the heart.'

These were influences that had skipped a generation – Bugg's musical diet was increasingly being drawn from the 1970s and, particularly, the 1960s. 'It's just good music,' he later told Nottingham's *LeftLion* website. 'When I listen to music from the sixties it makes my ears prick up, so when I first heard music from that era I thought that I wanted to try and write songs like those guys. I didn't want to copy them – I wanted to create my own sound, but in that style. My sound isn't a deliberate copy.'

In attempting to create his own sound, Bugg began to toy with writing his own songs, pulling influences from the songs and artists he was accumulating in his atypical record collection: 'I was about 14 years old,' he told website *The Daily Beast*. 'I was playing covers up until that point. And I thought: All these songs I really enjoy playing have all been written by these people themselves. And some of those songs could make your day – could tap into how you were feeling at that particular moment. And I thought: That is what I'd love to do – write songs that could help people or inspire people. Make somebody's day. That would be the best thing in the world.' One of his earliest efforts – if not his first – was called 'I See Her Crying' – described by Bugg as, 'three chords, kind of a mixture of country and Buddy Holly and a bit of blues. That was when I realised I could take all my influences – everything that I heard or loved – and put [them] into one thing.'

This strange mix of the new, the old – and the new which self-consciously refers back to the old – would be the starting point for Bugg's music career. His taste in 'old' music meant he was out of step with his hip-hop loving mates and he knew it: 'People ask me now if I had the mickey taken out of me for listening to that kind of music but it never happened,' he said. 'Not one person did. They just respected what I did and that probably helped me carry on.'

These are the key social and musical events that would shape Jake Bugg's future – but they would have a wider effect too. They would conspire to change the Nottingham music scene forever.

CHAPTER TWO

CAN WE
FIX IT?

Soundtrack:
Donovan – 'Catch the Wind' 1965
Ten Years After – 'Love Like a Man' 1970
Paper Lace – 'The Night Chicago Died' 1974

Nottingham has never been a city that has rested on its musical laurels – largely because, in some people's eyes, it's never really had any.

A one-hit wonder here, a novelty record there and a semi-successful band whose drummer went to university in the city – that has been the perception of Nottingham's contribution to the British music scene up until Jake Bugg's arrival.

It's a perception that those closely involved in the Nottingham scene are acutely aware of. 'See, that's the thing about Nottingham, it's always had a music scene but it's never had a *successful* music scene,' says Simon Wilson, entertainment editor of the *Nottingham Post*. 'It's been like a running joke for years and years. I mean, we know all about Manchester, Liverpool, Birmingham and Glasgow. We're not supposed to be in competition with them because we're not that size of city. But when you compare us to somewhere like Bristol or even our closest rivals – in terms of cities – Derby and Leicester... Leicester's got Kasabian and Mark Morrison; Derby [has] White Town, having a Number One hit. Over the years there's only been the odd credible act but never a scene – like Stereo MCs, for example. But Stereo MCs moved to London before they became Stereo MCs. It's like Tindersticks – they were the same; Nottingham lads, went down to London, formed Tindersticks. They were never purely Nottingham lads, like Jake Bugg is. He's born and bred.'

The story of Jake Bugg is now intertwined with the city so tightly that it's impossible to separate the two: if you're talking about Bugg, you're talking about Nottingham and its musical heritage. Or lack of it.

Pre-Bugg, the key local acts that the city has been able to point to have been a rum mix to say the least, something that Simon Wilson is all too aware of. 'Whenever we've been successful, it's always been embarrassing: like Su Pollard had a Number Two hit single and Alvin Stardust, who's from just over the way in Mansfield. Paper Lace, "Billy Don't Be a Hero". It was always quite naff stuff like that.'

Paper Lace were – prior to Bugg – the last Nottingham act

to get to Number One. The band had formed in Nottingham in the late 1960s and had released a smattering of singles with little impact. They entered TV talent show *Opportunity Knocks* in 1974 and won the chance to return to play on the following week's show for five weeks running. After the exposure, they were offered the song 'Billy Don't Be a Hero', a countrified slice of pop that tells the story of a Civil War soldier leaving his girl behind to join the army. It went to Number One in early 1974 and the band followed it up with two more UK hits in the same year. They also had a massive hit in the US with 'The Night Chicago Died', selling three million copies of the single. The band made a comeback of sorts in 1978, writing and performing 'We Got The Whole World In Our Hands' with Nottingham Forest FC.

Paper Lace became something of a touchstone in the story of Jake's success and that of the Nottingham music scene – every time the city's musical heritage was written about, Paper Lace were produced as the last example of real success. If you're writing about the story of Nottingham music, you need to include Paper Lace. 'I don't think, necessarily, we are a one-off, I don't think we're the best that Nottingham's got to offer in any way shape or form,' Paper Lace's lead singer Phil Wright told me. 'It's just that we were in the right place at the right time.'

As a 'talent show' act, Paper Lace's image was never cool, but that doesn't do their achievements justice. When 'Billy Don't Be a Hero' was at Number One, hits *really were* hits: 'People went out and spent their pocket money on their favourite acts and it was easy to chalk up 250,000 sales, which was a silver disc, and then 500,000, which got you a gold disc,' says Phil today. 'When our second hit went to Number One in the States, we got a platinum disc, which was to commemorate sales in excess of two million for a single. I mean that's selling single records – that is bumper times, when people did sell large numbers. EMI were our distributers, you could go to the factory and see your record being pumped out on a huge press. I remember visiting EMI at Hayes in Middlesex, going there and having a tour around the factory and six presses were banging out "Billy Don't Be a Hero" and one press was knocking out a single by Wings and Paul McCartney. I mean, it was an indication of how your record was selling, the number of presses that were actually producing the single.'

The city of Nottingham had never known musical success like it and embraced the band and their achievements: 'We had a big civic reception,' Phil recalls. 'We came back from London on the train from a television performance and we got off the train at the station and there was press and public just milling around – it was quite amazing. We were taken by Rolls Royce and they took us to the council building in the centre of Nottingham and we went up on the balcony and the city square was completely full of people. It was a bit fantastic and a bit mind blowing really. They've done that with lots of things that have happened to Nottingham. I remember when Nottingham Forest was winning everything in sight, they reacted in exactly the same way. I remember when [Nottingham skaters] Torvill and Dean had their success – they reacted in exactly the same way. The people of Nottingham are very supportive of home-grown local talent, it's just maybe they haven't had the opportunity to show that enthusiasm a lot.'

Paper Lace's success was huge but short-lived: 'Just after our success, punk came along and turned the music industry on its head. I think, since then, there has been a steady decline in the music industry and there [are] now very few outlets for new bands to sell their wares or get known. It's now very difficult for people from Nottingham – and other places – to actually get out there and get themselves known. The music industry now is a completely different animal to what it was when we were around in the mid-seventies.'

History has been a little unfair on Paper Lace and the band's achievements – but there have been other pockets of credibility and success in Nottingham's musical history. The late Alvin Lee – guitarist with blues rockers Ten Years After – was a Nottingham lad and the band had a run of critically acclaimed albums in the late 1960s and early 1970s. But for an indication of how desperate things were, *Hi-Di-Hi* actress Su Pollard is claimed as part of Nottingham's musical history after she scored a Number Two hit with her single 'Starting Together' in 1986.

Paper Lace's success hung so heavily over some people in Nottingham that a Facebook campaign was started in 2008 to get a local act back to the top of the charts. The page was started by another key person in the Bugg story, Mark Del. The ebullient Del is the man behind *NUSIC*, a website and podcast that is evangelical about new Nottingham music – hence the title. 'When the page was started it seemed, frankly, like a rather stupid notion in certain quarters, causing some people to post abusive messages on the site. If you look at the page you'll see some mardy [angry] stuff on it – it's not pleasant,' Del told me.

Pedantic types even took the time to point out that Nottingham had actually scored a Number One since Paper Lace: Nottingham's very own Paul K. Joyce wrote 'Can We Fix It' for the *Bob the Builder* series and the single went to the top of the charts in the year 2000. What they wanted was a *credible* Number One. 'The argument was that Nottingham hadn't produced a Number One for forty years,' says Del. 'I really don't care what happened in the seventies. If "Billy Don't Be A Hero" is the best you can offer me, that says it all. And people were going, "What about Tindersticks? What about KWRS? Wasn't one of them from Nottingham?" The moment you start trying to claim people as local musicians, that says it all. That's the thing with Jake. He's Nottingham and proud. Now people want to shout about it. People are now claiming to be from Nottingham when they're not. We have to check.'

Tindersticks and their swampy, indie blues were the critics' darling in the 1990s. Led by Stuart A. Staples, they released a series of singles and albums that went down better with reviewers than they did with the record-buying public and their biggest hit 'Bathtime' reached Number 38 in 1997. 'Tindersticks *have* done some cool things,' Del concedes. 'In terms of acts that can claim a link? Spiritualized, The Klaxons, Friendly Fires – there [have] been quite a lot of acts who've had some of their members go to one of the unis or something like that. But the moment you have to focus on those bands shows the lack of things that have happened. In 2008 Nottingham had failed – it was like an Alcoholics Anonymous thing, we've got to admit our failings first before we can address them. So admitting Nottingham had failed, admitting that actually our musicians do want to succeed. Nottingham has underachieved – what can be done about this? At that time, I was angry. I was militant. This lack of success, this lack of willingness to help musicians – I pissed some people off in the process. It was an absolute disgrace that the only thing we could point back to was Paper Lace... and to try and claim bands like Showaddywaddy. That was the best we could do.'

BBC presenter Dean Jackson – the man who gave airplay to Jake's mum and dad and would do the same for the young Bugg – also paints a picture of an underperforming Nottingham music scene: 'I think there's always been a decent music scene in Nottingham but it's never been very fashionable. By that I mean, in terms of what the A&R scouts were looking for in London, it was never really quite right. I mean what was going on around that time in the early nineties was... [there was a] lot of kind of mutant jazz going on, that kind of thing. Then there was the Earache record label, which was very heavy music – that was based in Nottingham. There was a lot of music around at that time but it wasn't very marketable. So I think the A&R people just gave up on Nottingham to a large extent.'

Nottingham is, of course, in the Midlands – and, in musical terms, the Midlands means metal. Black Sabbath, Led Zeppelin, Judas Priest, Diamond Head, Napalm Death... all forged in the industrial heartland of the Midlands. 'Nottingham's got a big metal scene,' confirms Rock City DJ Rob Upton. 'They love the classics, plus they love nu metal – Limp Bizkit, Papa Roach. Pop punk is a massive thing in Nottingham. The one thing we don't play a lot of is indie – people just walk off the dance floor. Indie is more introverted, it doesn't really work in the rock scene. The main scene was metal and punk – black metal and tech metal. There was a band I was in called Sanzen, there was Earthtone 9, and a band called Iron Monkey who were hard-core punk. Don Bronco were at university and made it onto the cover of *Kerrang!* Baby Godzilla have come from the punk scene and are doing really well. There [were] always bands around but no one really big. Before Jake Bugg came out there was a spate of bluesy kind of bands – not the Dylan blues but proper, dirty blues. Like Royston Ducksford and a band called Haggard Cat Bothday Present. There's loads of people doing their own thing in their own little quarter – making demos in their bedrooms.'

So there it is – a picture of the Nottingham scene that forms the background to the story of Jake Bugg. While all this is going on, the teenage Jake is still in his bedroom, picking out the chords of songs that have caught his ear and even starting to write a few of his own. 'I was playing cover versions of things at 14 or 15 and that taught me about songs, how they fit together, their structure and melody,' Jake later told *Spotify* (the digital music service). 'I learned from them. The first songs I wrote weren't that great but some I still play. I have old demos of some really rough, terrible recordings!'

'I remember him writing songs like "Country Song" in his bedroom,' mum Leeysa later told the BBC. 'He'd come downstairs and be like, "Mum, what do you think of this, do you think it's all right?" I'd get so emotional I couldn't even look at him. I'd have to turn away. I'd have tears pouring down my face.'

Although he took music at school, Jake would later be highly critical of the way music was taught to him, with its concentration on theory over practical playing: 'I failed my GCSE music theory test,' he told the *NME* in 2013. 'Teachers should be giving kids guitars, giving them instruments instead of teaching them what a fucking semi-quaver is. It might be useful to know but it's not what is really important: music comes from the soul. Even if it's just three chords, if you're being honest and singing about something that means something to you, that's what music is about.'

Despite Don McLean's insistence he should 'stay in school', he struggled to fit in academically. Outside of school Bugg was no angel but existed just on the periphery of getting into real trouble. 'I did other things kids do, go egging windows, it was funny,' he later told XFM. 'I remember a woman chased me for ages all around the block. I remember being quite scared for ages, didn't know what was going to happen. But as I started getting a bit older, going out drinking, going out in town… But I couldn't really afford to do that stuff, so that's when I started spending more time in my bedroom, writing songs.'

Bugg says it was his mates, rather than he himself, who got in trouble with the law, but he was nearly arrested aged 14 when he went drinking in a field with his cousins. Spotting the cops, he gently dropped his stash of lager in the grass – the police had no evidence so couldn't do anything. He began smoking dope and remembers his first 'white out' after smoking too much: 'One of the worst nights of my life,' he later told journalist Simon Goddard. 'I was round some random guy's house on the estate. It wasn't a very nice flat and I drank too much and smoked too much and my cousin had to take me home. It was fucking horrendous!'

So in his own free time, Bugg was like most kids his age on the estate. Back in school though, he was rapidly coming to the conclusion that education wasn't for him. In fact, it was Bugg's behaviour at school that inadvertently brought about his conversion from bedroom guitar player to performer. He'd been put in 'isolation' from his classmates and was told that the only way he could get out of it was to perform at the school concert. Aged 14, Jake was about to play live for the first time: 'My first ever gig on a proper stage was probably at secondary school,' he told the *Contact Music* website, 'which is one of the scariest gigs you can do – all the rest of the school, the same people you're gonna see for the next three or four years...'

Sitting in his bedroom before the school show, Bugg surely would have been tempted to do a current song, a song that everyone in the school would be aware of. But Jake stuck to his guns musically and chose a song that his peers were almost certain to be unfamiliar with, by an artist they'd probably never heard of: 'Catch the Wind' by Donovan. Released in 1965, it's one of the British singer's most Dylanesque songs – it's reflective, melancholy yet loving. It was the flower-power troubadour's first single and was a Number Four hit. If you were a teenage lad getting ready to perform at a school concert, it's probably the last song you would choose to sing in front of your mates. But that's exactly what Bugg did.

The performance went so well that many of his school friends said he should audition for TV talent show *Britain's Got Talent*. Even so, soon after his first 'gig', he was adamant that going down that route wasn't for him – he'd never do that because it wouldn't feel 'genuine' or 'natural'.

'Everyone was supportive,' Jake later said when recalling the performance. 'No one ever said a bad word, luckily enough for me. No one ever put me down. So, yeah, I thought: If I could do that, I could do nearly anything.'

CHAPTER THREE

WHO THE HELL IS *THIS*?

Soundtrack:
Cockney Rejects – 'I'm Not a Fool' 1979
Bad Manners – 'Special Brew' 1980
The Swiines – 'Stonefaced' 2010

With his first gig under his belt, Jake Bugg decided to make inroads into the local live-music scene. But he quickly realised that he'd have to go beyond Clifton to find places to play: 'I'm not aware of any Clifton scene,' says Mark Del of Nottingham new music website *NUSIC* and one of Jake's earliest musical supporters. 'I'm not aware of any venues – there are a few pubs. The thing about the Nottingham scene is that the hub is totally based around the city centre. There's no part of Nottingham that's more than 15 minutes from the city centre. If you're looking for structural reasons for the

Nottingham scene – physical things – one of them is that you have this vibrant city and you can stand in Market Square and be a ten minute walk from the world's best bands playing at Rock City, ten minutes from The Maze, where Jake played in his early days, and ten minutes from the world's biggest pop stars at the arena. I'm from London – there's nowhere like that in London. If you go to the O2, you've got a fifty-quid cab ride to get back into the West End. Nottingham's pretty unique. It allows these interconnections and this spontaneity and interactions between the venues and the musicians.'

One of the first sets of doors that the young Jake Bugg knocked on were the red ones outside the Forest Tavern on Mansfield Road. Despite what Mark Del might have you believe, the pub is just at the edge of Nottingham city centre, a good 15-minute uphill walk from the main shopping area. At the back of the pub is The Maze, a former function room that's now a gig-space. Folk and roots acts go down well at The Maze, as do punk and ska acts from back in the day – the walls are plastered with posters for the likes of Bad Manners and the Cockney Rejects. 'Jake's introduction to Nottingham was playing a venue called The Maze, which is a classic, underground, dirty toilet venue,' says Mark Del. 'I don't mean that nastily – it's how they'd describe themselves. He was playing there around 2009, 2010. Of course he's very young at this point.'

'The Maze is an underground club really,' Maze manager Gaz Peacham told me after I'd made the trek and walked up Mansfield Road – in the pouring rain – to the venue. 'It's separated into two places really, so you've got the Forest Tavern at the front, a sort of old-school ale house. Then in the back we've changed it from a function room into a music venue and it's a very earthy place, I guess a rootsy place. We get touring bands in; it tends to be a lot of rootsy music, folk, reggae acts, stuff like that and we've always had a very large focus on local bands so we do local-band nights several times a week. It's sort of your local venue for local acts, I guess.

'The venue is classed as being in Forest Fields, we are just within the city limits. You've got to walk up a fairly large hill, so it's an effort to get here in a way. It's not like one of these places where people are walking around town having a few drinks or on a pub crawl and say, "Let's go there." You've got to make a decision to come to The Maze, so I think most people that come here come here specifically for the music most of the time. The thing with Nottingham is it's got a very varied scene. It's not like you come to Nottingham and every pub's putting on indie-folky acts in a similar style to Jake. It's got a very varied scene anyway, there [are] lots of good hip-hop acts, good "dancey" acts and more heavier rock acts. It's got a great metal scene and it's got a great hip-hop scene. The underground hip-hop scene has actually been quite big for close to ten years now, so there's been a lot of stuff going on there.'

Although Gaz Peacham didn't realise it at the time, Bugg had been to The Maze as an audience member, before the teen-ager played at the venue himself: 'The first time I met Jake, he came to The Maze because his cousin Scott, who's in a band called The Swiines, was playing and Jake came along to watch,' Peacham told me. 'Jake was really young at the time. He was actually with a relative and they said, "Is it all right to bring this lad in? He's only 12 or 13 – is he all right to come along to the gig? He's the cousin of the singer of the band." And that's when I first met him and remembered him coming here.'

In later years, Jake would credit The Swiines as a key influence. Describing themselves as 'psychedelic/garage', the band have a swirly Britpop swagger along the lines of Oasis spliced with The Charlatans. They had formed from the ashes of two separate local acts: The Bets and The Arcane. Lead singer Scott Bugg looks a lot like Jake only with better cheekbones and they share that Gallagheresque, nasal way of singing. Scott Bugg would return the favour of his cousin's support and would be regularly seen at Jake's early gigs. At one stage Jake even 'joined' The Swiines: 'I played bass for them for a few gigs,' Jake later explained in an interview with Mark Del. 'The bass player left so I played with them.'

Six months after Jake saw The Swiines at The Maze, Gaz Peacham got an email from the teenager asking if he could perform there: 'He'd started to play the guitar, he'd been to The Maze to see his cousin play and he was interested in getting a gig. We've always had a policy that we're not going to stop younger people playing... or older people, for that matter. If we think it's good, that's it – and certainly if it's local music. We're very into supporting local acts. We gave Jake a slot on "Notts in a Nutshell", our local-band night. We do four or five a month, where it's just strictly local bands, most of the time quite young, new bands from Nottinghamshire. And he came down and played one of those.'

Peacham knew that Jake was young – but was shocked when Bugg turned up to play his first gig at The Maze: 'I vividly remember the first ever gig Jake played here because he was *tiny*. He was a young lad, really young – and he's not a big lad anyway. I think he's grown out a bit now but he wasn't a big lad in stature to start with. He was always quite shy and slightly reclusive and I remember him coming in – I was downstairs when he walked through the door – and he just had his guitar on his back with no case and he was wearing a tracksuit and I thought: Who the hell is *this*?'

Peacham's expectations of the tiny musician weren't high. He initially didn't bother to watch as the youngster began to play, despite the fact that he lived in a flat above the venue. That quickly changed: 'I was upstairs when he actually played, upstairs in my flat,' he says. 'My girlfriend manages the pub with me and she books a lot of the acts and it was her that booked Jake initially. She had been downstairs watching him and she came upstairs to get me and said, "This young lad is playing, you should come down and watch him, he's got an amazing voice. He's not the greatest guitarist ever but he's got an amazing voice and he only looks 13 or 14." I knew he was really young, so I came down and watched him and I thought: This lad's got something good, he could really be something in a few years. I never quite thought he'd do as much as he has! But from that very first gig, I remember people saying, "For a lad of his age, he's got something there, he's really good."'

Jake himself had another reason to remember the gig: 'The promoter gave me a tenner for doing it,' he later told journalist Simon Wilson. 'Which was nice, because I didn't have the bus fare to get back home.'

The Jake Bugg who is now known internationally was beginning to take shape on the stages of The Maze and other Nottingham venues: the lack of fuss, the non-existent stage patter, the stripped-down, no-nonsense approach: 'It's always been a raw sound and I think that's the way Jake probably likes it,' says Peacham. 'He always was a raw sort of character anyway, turning up with his guitar on his back, with no case. I remember several gigs where he'd turn up ten minutes before he was about to play. Wouldn't bother sound-checking or anything, he'd just show up and play. [He] was always quite a natural: "I'm here to play and that's what's it's all about." He's not one of those characters that chatted too much on stage or hung around for hours before and after networking – for Jake there was always a large focus [on] playing his music.'

The Nottingham gig scene and its supportive, nurturing atmosphere proved to be the ideal place for the young Jake to play and learn his craft. He learned something else too: that tenner he got first time around was not going to be a regular occurrence. 'These gigs are basically a chance to play in a proper venue with a proper sound system – they're non-paying gigs,' says Peacham. 'We charge a couple of quid in, people bring their friends and families down and it's a chance for them to learn their chops and a chance for us to see them.

There was a good underground scene, very communal scene for five to ten years before Jake's album went to Number One.'

Jake began to eke out gigs as and when he could find them. He'd often dash back from school, sling his guitar on his back and get a bus into town. 'I played a few Monday night gigs in the little bar at the Rescue Rooms after school,' he later recalled in an interview with the *Nottingham Post*. 'People were eating their dinner and not taking much notice. I was probably wearing a tracksuit – maybe that freaked them out.'

Another early appearance that generated a ripple of interest was at The Chameleon venue in September 2009. This much-loved arts centre closed in the summer of 2013. Bugg – as ever at this stage appearing early on in the evening – supported the likes of jazzy guitarist Howard Miles and electronic four-piece Tom For Idea. His performance merited a mention in Nottingham listings magazine and website *LeftLion*. Reviewer Alistair Catterall wrote, 'The first one to really check out was Jake Bugg. Set quietly down in the corner of the bar, this small-in-stature-and-presence musician really lets out when he plays. From his own material to a wild "Universal Soldier" [a Buffy Sainte-Marie song covered by Donovan], there is an intensity here not seen since the folk radicalism of the 1960s. Peering out from under dark eyes, he played, then got up and left without a word. There was an understated strength to his performance, with influences ranging from Dylan to [US protest singer Phil] Ochs. If we ever feel like returning to our city's roots and burning the castle down once again, Jake Bugg needs to be leading the procession.'

All in all a pretty good review for a 15-year-old – not only that, this review was also one of the earliest occasions that Bugg's name was linked to Bob Dylan. It wouldn't be the last time that Jake's name appeared in the same sentence as the folk legend. Dylan had forged his reputation as the chronicler of social change and upheaval in 1960s America, producing a string of albums that still feature on many critics' Top Ten lists. His shift to an electric sound in the mid-1960s led to him being accused of being a 'Judas' by folk purists but his name looms large over popular music, particularly in the US. Dylan's name would become almost magnetically attached to Bugg's over the coming years, as an easy shorthand to describe Jake's sound as well as his look and attitude.

These early Nottingham gigs were often sparsely attended affairs with Jake playing to the staff and a few friends and relatives. It stayed that way for some time: 'Regularly, he'd play to hardly anyone,' recalls Gaz Peacham. 'They weren't busy gigs here really. That's an interesting thing, people always think: Oh, Jake Bugg played here ten times in 2009 and 2010, they must have been great shows. Well a lot of them were, some of them were seventy-five to eighty per cent full, when there was a good line-up with him and a few other acts on, but a lot of them he was playing to ten people – some of them were probably less than that; just to his family and a few friends. There were plenty of gigs where Jake would have been playing to hardly anyone here, but I think he learned his trade doing that and he kept doing it and he learned from every single gig and he crafted his art and refined it and hence he got to where he got.'

Undaunted by the sparse audiences, Bugg became a familiar sight around Clifton and the city centre – a young man in a tracksuit, guitar on his back (it was a while until he got a case for it) heading off in search of open-mic nights and pubs that would allow him to play. Not everyone was as welcoming as Gaz Peacham: 'Some of them would be like, "Don't be daft, you're 15, you're not coming in the pub,"' Bugg later told *Shortlist* magazine. 'But then some places gave me a couple of slots and people saw my face a bit more. I did that for a couple of years before I got signed. The crowds were hit and miss but it gave me that experience.'

Jake's dad David – despite being a musician himself – says that he didn't know about his son's nocturnal activities on the local music scene: 'I had no idea when he started playing gigs in Nottingham because he was too young to be in these places,' he later told the *Nottingham Post*. 'I think his mum was worried how I'd react but, when I found out, she assured me he was fine.'

Gaz Peacham of The Maze says, 'There was a point when Jake was playing here at least once a month – there was a good six-month run of that I think. Initially, he'd start on these sort of open-mic shows. I know he played a few support shows to touring artists here a bit later down the line. He also started playing a few of our acoustic nights and folk nights, more specifically aimed at the crowd that we felt he'd appeal to.'

In the summer of 2009 Jake played his first ever festival and also got his first mention in the local newspaper. He played at the bottom of the bill at the Parklive event at Vernon Park in Basford, north Nottingham. The free event was organised by the city council, the Greater Nottinghamshire Partnership and local label Arboretum Records. Arboretum's Nick McDonald – now a Nottingham city councillor – told me about the event: 'We put the Parklive gig on at Vernon Park in August 2009. We did put Jake on at that event. He was only fifteen, I think, so it probably was one of his first gigs. The event was a free, all-day, live-music event. It was quite small and held under a large marquee but I guess we probably had over a thousand people there over the course of the day. From memory, Jake was the first act on that day and played very well. It was obvious he had talent even then.'

In the run-up to the event, Jake got his first mention in the *Nottingham Post*. It wouldn't be the last. 'Funk group The Apples will be headlining the event,' the short article said. 'Local acts include Dan Beswick, Jake Bugg, Tim McDonald, Damon Downs, Becky Syson, Chris McDonald, Hhymn, Lois, Old Basford, Fat Digester and The Rugged Sound System. The event will start at 11am with workshops in salsa drumming and ukulele playing before the music starts at noon.'

NUSIC's Mark Del attended the festival but admits he

didn't arrive in time to catch the young Bugg: 'It went on from the afternoon into the evening. The Apples headlined. They were good. Anyone who says they saw Jake there and it was amazing is being mischievous. No one told me about him after that gig. There's a decent group of people out there who would tell us if they saw someone fabulous.'

Despite being free, everyone who played got paid, although Nick McDonald recalls there was a slight issue with Jake's money: 'All the acts were paid a small amount of money. I recall that we paid him a cheque made out to "Jake Bugg" and his mum rang us the next day to say that for whatever reason he couldn't cash the cheque and asked if we could pay him in cash instead! I think my colleague had to meet her in town the next day. Anyway, the event was a success, it finished with The Apples, who are a fantastic live act, and actually quite a few gigs we did over that period featured artists who have gone on to bigger and better things. I think it's fair to say that whole period was a turning point for the Nottingham music scene, with a lot of talent coming through, and a variety of event promoters really pushing the local scene. Certainly, the growing success of Nottingham's current music scene owes a fair amount to that period I think.'

As well as solo shows like the Parklive event, Jake also started playing with other bands – some of them very short-lived – at the same time as developing his solo act. Despite the fact that he had, by this stage, just turned 16, he was a prolific live musician. One band he played with were The

Rubiks, a distinctly heavier proposition than Bugg's solo material. The four-piece band – with Bugg cutting an Alex Turneresque figure with his white Stratocaster guitar – was a short-lived proposition around the summer of 2010. He also played with a band called DAX. Gaz Peacham of The Maze says, 'Rubiks played here and DAX as well – they didn't last long. Jake would be in a band for six months, then be in the next one for three months. He played bass in a couple of local bands as well, doing sessions for slightly older lads and mates. Jake was one of these people, at first, that every time I met him, he'd have a new band and there was probably a year or so where that happened until he decided, "Right, I'm going to start concentrating on the solo stuff." But even then, when he started doing the solo and doing the kind of music we know him for now, he was still hopping from band to band. At some point he must have realised that the solo stuff was working and that was where he wanted to go – and that he was getting the attention doing the solo stuff, more than the band stuff.'

The other aspect of Bugg's musical persona that was evident from the very start was his work ethic. 'He was really proactive,' recalls Gaz Peacham. 'He was one of those guys that did work ridiculously hard when he first started. I'm sure he still does. He was always very hard working – he used to play here once a month at least and when you include his bands, probably twice a month. So he was probably playing here more than any other person in Nottingham at one point I imagine, or certainly on par with anyone else. At the same time, he was also playing down at ten other venues each month in town.'

Throughout 2010 Jake's name popped up on more and more open-mic nights and acoustic gigs: he appeared at the bottom of the bill at The Alley Cafe in the city centre, supporting the likes of Undercats and Beatmasta Bill Cooper. He played support slots at the Acoustickle night, where he got a rave billing despite his lowly place on the bill: 'Jake Bugg – he's probably the best performer in the ways of voice and style and presence... and he's 15,' the publicity said. 'It's a haunting Nick Cave meets sixties rebel guitarists at a mining strike. I love it.' He even played an arts-and-crafts evening called 'Jumpers For Goalposts' where – in honour of his surname – guests were invited to create a piece of art to represent a famous person crossed with an insect. Suggestions included Bugsy Malone, Marty McFly and rock band The Scorpions.

Jake Bugg may still have been at school but he was, in reality, on an apprenticeship scheme of his own making. By the summer of 2010 he was becoming a fixture on the scene. Gaz Peacham of The Maze: 'There was a good year when he was playing here very regularly, but in that year he was also playing Nottingham in general very regularly. Jake was probably playing a gig a week at that point in Nottingham, learning his trade. Every time you saw him, he was getting slightly better on his guitar, slightly more refined and his performances were getting better and better and he was starting to get a buzz about him. Then he started to get on the local radio shows, getting a bit of press about him, especially about his age and being so young. He worked ridiculously hard, he was playing a lot and there wasn't a week that went by when I went on Facebook or walked around town and there wasn't a poster or a Facebook event without Jake's name on somewhere. Every week he had a gig in Nottingham, every single week without fail, for a good year or two. You make your own luck really, and I think Jake certainly did that, he worked very hard and then when he got the opportunities he took them with both hands.'

As well as his incessant gigging, three key events involving the local press and radio shows would prove vital to the development of Jake Bugg's future. One was with BBC Nottingham; another was the *Notts Unsigned Future Sessions* podcast. But the first was a short video he made for the *Nottingham Post*. It would lead directly to him acquiring a manager and, ultimately, getting a record deal. The success that Jake has generated can be traced back to the very first session and interview he did for *This Is Music*.

CHAPTER FOUR

HE SEEMS REALLY COOL, LET'S GET HIM ON

Soundtrack:
Jay Hart – 'Time On Our Hands' 2009
The Drums – 'Let's Go Surfing' 2009
The Swiines – 'Love is Blind' 2013

The *Nottingham Post* – formerly known as the *Nottingham Evening Post* – has a long and illustrious history of covering Nottinghamshire and aspects of its neighbouring counties stretching back to 1878. It's a big patch with plenty to go at but, as we've already heard, the lack of musical success for acts from the area meant that pickings could be pretty slim in terms of the paper's coverage of music. The artists the paper wrote about would often generate local interest but they didn't seem to translate to the wider UK scene. When they did, they weren't viewed as being credible. That would change when 16-year-old Jake Bugg approached the paper after hearing that the *Post*'s entertainment section was looking for acts. Now they have plenty to write about: 'There is never enough Jake Bugg,' says the *Post*'s Simon Wilson about the paper's attitude towards the singer today. 'We'll just keep doing it and doing it.'

Nottingham Post video-journalist Zoe Kirk was the person behind the idea to film local acts for the paper's *EG* (Entertainment Guide) section. She'd also coerce national and international acts to come in and be interviewed and the likes of Tinie Tempah, The Drums and James Blunt have also appeared on *This Is Live*. The show would provide the first of many appearances for Jake Bugg in the pages of the *Post* and in its online content. *EG* editor Simon Wilson said, 'The first time that we, as a paper, experienced Jake was on an online video thing that we used to do called *This Is Live*. Zoe Kirk came up with this idea of profiling local artists and local musicians once a week. Just get them in, have a quick chat, playing one song, edit it together, five minutes tops. Zoe's no longer with us. She's not dead, she left the paper!'

'We'd feature all kinds of different bands and musicians,' recalls Zoe Kirk, alive and well and now running her own production company. 'It wasn't a particular type – anyone who was writing their own original music and wanted to appear on the show. It was a real mix. It wasn't like we just picked the best ones! It was supposed to be an open opportunity for all Nottingham artists. Because it was weekly and it ran for four years, can you imagine how many acts we needed to get on? At first we thought it was going to be really tricky but, in actual fact, we were inundated. Nottingham had a huge, huge music scene, much bigger than we thought when we first started to do it, so it wasn't ever a problem finding artists. In terms of big stars, there hasn't been a whole barrage of big acts yet. It's just one of those things that out of the great talent that Nottingham has, none of these have managed to be spotted or hit the big time.'

Until Jake Bugg that is.

Zoe Kirk described to me the usual process for recording an appearance: 'They would be interviewed – usually it was down at the Stealth club at the Rescue Rooms venue in Nottingham. They'd have a chat about their interest in music, where it came from, how their style had evolved and so on. Then they would perform one acoustic track live for us, which they'd perform a couple of times so we could film angles for the edit.'

Among the singers who applied to be on *This Is Live* was 16-year-old Jake Bugg from Clifton: 'Jake got in touch with me himself,' Zoe told me. 'His cousin Scott Bugg is in The Swiines, another band from Nottingham, and that band were on the show a few months prior. I think Jake must have seen it and thought it would be great to do the same thing. He was only 16 at the time when he got in touch. He was playing a few gigs around Nottingham – I think he'd played The Maze a couple of times and he was just starting to perform live around town. He got in touch with us and said he'd like to do it. He sent me a link to a video he'd done at The Maze; one that they'd recorded of him on stage. I thought: Yeah, he seems really cool, let's get him on.'

The paper ran a short piece to flag up the youngster's appearance on *This Is Live*: 'Folk-rock singer-songwriter Jake Bugg, from Clifton, is next to perform live and chat to Zoe Kirk on the Stealth sofa for our weekly video showcase. The 16-year-old comes from a musical family. He takes inspiration from seeing his older cousin, Scott Bugg, fronting Nottingham rock band The Swiines. Consequently, Jake, who had always played solo, recently formed his own band, Rubiks.'

Jake's appearance on *This Is Live* – the first interview and session of his career – is a fascinating watch in the context of his current success. Up for discussion were 1960s influences, his parents electro-pop career and the first song he ever wrote: 'Can't remember it exactly,' he tells Kirk. 'It's probably shocking though. I think I was about 14 and I recorded it on my mate's laptop. It wasn't very good quality but I still listen to it now and again.' He even mentioned he'd had the chance to meet one of his heroes. 'I went to see Don McLean. He had a gig in Sheffield, he came out after and I got to meet him.'

Zoe Kirk would be the first to discover – but certainly not the last – that Bugg is not the most gushing of interviewees. 'It was his first interview as far as I could tell,' she recalls. 'He doesn't chat outrageously as you probably know from his character anyway. But this was his first interview at the

44

age of 16 and yes, he was quite stilted and quite shy. But he still came across as a lovely guy, a very nice chap – just not used to being interviewed.'

A shoelace from a trainer is attached to the neck of his Yamaha acoustic guitar – it appears to have been acting as guitar strap but isn't needed here as the teenager is sitting down. Resplendent in a green and purple shell-suit top and jeans, he's introduced by Zoe Kirk as '16-year-old singer-songwriter, Jake Bugg' and picks and strums his way through 'Fallin'', sung in a tremulous but very loud voice. It's one of Jake's early 'baby girl, I love you' songs, the twist being that she's been doing him wrong rather the other way round. He'd been playing the song live and it had gone down well when he'd sung it at The Maze. 'I wrote it in my bedroom,' he told Zoe Kirk during the *This Is Live* interview. 'I just came up with the picking pattern and then I put the chorus to it. I played it at school a couple of times and I got good feedback.'

The awkwardness of 'Bugg the interviewee' then melted away as 'Bugg the musician' shone through. 'He seemed quite shy, so we did the interview first and then we went to record his first take of his music performance and it was literally one of these jaw-dropping moments,' Kirk told me. 'He just seemed so confident, a completely different guy when he is singing. Really confident, amazing sound. We were really blown away – you could tell there was something special there. In the interview he seemed really shy and I was concerned at how comfortable he'd feel performing in front of us and filming as well with him not used to it but no, such a different guy when he picked up his guitar and started singing – it was incredible.'

Not everyone was quite as knocked out as Zoe Kirk was by Jake's debut – those doubters included *EG* editor Simon Wilson, who knew that anyone and everyone was allowed a shot at a *This Is Live* slot, meaning the quality could be variable. Wilson says, 'There was loads to choose from. Seriously, she was booked up a year in advance with people wanting to be on it. Zoe would do one a week and there was no choosing – if you wanted to be on it, you could be on it. She'd obviously check them out and make sure that they weren't mental or something... because some were! But now and again she'd say, "Oh, have you seen this?" I used to watch each one every week – I'm probably the only one that did – and she said, "Oh, this one's really good." And it was Jake when he was 16. I didn't feel anything from it, I just thought: Oh, it's just another young lad with a guitar. Every now and again there would be someone on there and I'd think: Oh, excellent, that's really good... and you'd never hear from them again. But she did point that one out and he came back and did another one about a year later and it seemed to kick off after that. But at the time there was nothing. Nobody in the office was getting excited about it, saying, "Oh, we've discovered this." Obviously, we say that now!'

But there was one person who was excited by Jake's performance – very excited indeed. Local musician Jason Hart – known to all as Jay – saw the video and liked what he saw. Zoe Kirk: 'After the performance went up on the website, Jason Hart saw him on the video and clearly liked it. I knew Jay, as he'd been on *This is Live* a year or two previously and we'd also filmed a music video for him. So I knew Jay from meeting him a couple of times and I think he just carried on watching my little web show after his appearance, just to see what Nottingham artists were doing. He spotted Jake and got in touch with me. He may have rung me and I gave him an email address. He spotted Jake, took him under his wing, took him to his recording studio and began recording stuff with him.'

'Yes, it started with *This Is Live*,' Jake later confirmed. 'Jay saw it and got in touch. He invited me to his studio and we got on really well.'

Zoe Kirk is one of many people who believe that Hart's appearance in Bugg's story is one of the key elements of his later success: 'Jay Hart has been amazing for him,' she told me. 'They were really good friends from the start, which really helped Jake, because he was young and did need some guidance. He wasn't loud, obnoxious or PR-y, it's not how he is. So with a bit of help from Jay, who does know a few people and did have a recording studio, it really helped push him and helped in terms of getting him out there. A lot of the Nottingham artists are unsigned and don't have managers – I think that Jay's help must have made a difference.'

Hart had already experienced a varied career as a guitarist-for-hire session man and a solo artist. He'd toured with Spiritualized, the trippy rock band formed by Jason

Pierce from the quite-near-Nottingham town of Rugby and formed a band with ex-Lighthouse Family member Paul Tucker called The Orange Lights. By way of proof of his versatility, Hart has also played with country stars like Billie Jo Spears and Stella Parton – sister of Dolly. Good looking and personable – though perhaps lacking a truly distinctive singing voice – Hart was a proper musician, just as happy playing at a party thrown by singing legend Shirley Bassey as he was touring America or gigging in Nottingham. 'It started with busking and then playing in working-men's clubs, to playing in bars and then parties and weddings to radio and television and festivals,' Hart told Zoe Kirk in 2009, when he appeared on her web show to talk about a solo album he'd recorded. 'It's hard work and it has cost me in many ways but that's the life I chose. I can't complain, that's for sure! If Notts people realised just how much music is used commercially that comes from this town I think they would be amazed. There really is a great, supported network here, from the covers bands to the original bands. I'm a bit baffled as to why Nottingham hasn't "done a Manchester" – it's certainly got more than enough muscle to pull it off.'

Hart seemed to be tiring of life on the road and to be looking for fresh challenges: 'I got a bit tired of bands and horrible rehearsal rooms with warm cans of beer on Sunday mornings,' he said, just over a year before spotting Jake on the *Nottingham Post* video. 'I do go out occasionally with a band. I'm really into the idea of having a flexible band, sometimes just me, other nights maybe a pianist and a pedal steel player and some gospel singers. That kind of flexibility really switches me on at the moment. I can't stand generic churned out major label over-produced rubbish. My main gripe is "landfill" indie, average bands with average singers. I love it when something comes along and blows my socks off.'

Hart's socks were clearly blown off by Jake's performance of 'Fallin''. 'I thought he was the best thing I'd seen in twenty years,' he later told the *Nottingham Post*. 'The most amazing voice and most amazing songs.'

The *This Is Live* video would change the lives of both Bugg and the man who would become his manager: 'Jason has had his life transformed because he wasn't an established manager,' says Mark Del of *NUSIC*, who would also give Bugg an early and important break. 'I think Jason is really key to Jake's success – more than your average manager. Believing in Jake from a very early stage, taking a risk when he didn't really have the resources – he wasn't rich, he wasn't already connected – so he took a big risk on Jake. His manager has gone through a rise to fame as a manager at the same time as Jake has as an artist. His manager was a session musician playing in wedding bands. Now he's managing one of the hottest artists in the country and he's one of the hottest managers in the country.'

Jake now had his first interview and his first music session under his belt. He also had a handy video clip that he could send to other people interested in booking him. Another picture is now beginning to emerge – that of Bugg, the young mover and shaker, a 16-year-old with ambition. Not quite the shy, tongue-tied troubadour we may have expected. On leaving school he signed up for a music-tech course – it was to be short-lived: 'Did I learn anything?' he later told *The Guardian*. 'Yeah. I learned not to go there.'

Bugg had quickly become disenchanted with the way music was taught at school – now he managed to build up an aversion to the college course's take on how to get on in the music industry from day one. 'I just didn't find anything of the things they were teaching me to be true or relevant to the real music industry, you know?' he later explained to journalist John Lanham. 'It was just bullshit, man, and it was totally unnecessary. And the people who were teaching you were usually people who'd had a little taste of it themselves, but don't really know how it works. So my worst day there was when they had me designing a poster for a festival. And I thought: This isn't teaching us how to become better players or musicians or anything! It wasn't giving me any insight at all.'

The insight came from playing live and Bugg would later cite the 'apprenticeship' he served at these early gigs as being invaluable – lessons he learned are still of use to him today: 'I was gigging by the time I'd gone to that technology course,' he later explained to the *Face Culture* video channel. 'You're playing in front of a room – it might be ten people who don't have a clue who you are – that helps you develop your stagecraft because you're looking at people's reactions and what songs they react to a little bit more. Still to this day I have to deal with situations I've never had to deal with before – I had one girl collapse right in front of me and I had to stop. I had to get some help for this lady. I didn't know what to do. I've had guys fighting. You have to learn things... how to deal with certain situations.'

Quitting the course a matter of weeks after he started, the teenager clearly believed that he could learn more on the stages of The Maze and other venues than he could at college. His quiet demeanour clearly hid a strong desire to succeed. 'Even though he was a quiet lad, he'd always seemed to get in on things,' recalls Gaz Peacham of The Maze. 'You'd see him working with other acts, turning up at the right gigs and the right places. He might not say a lot and he might sit at the back but I think he was taking it all in. I think he pushed it in the right way – I don't know if that was a conscious thing or being a bit lucky. I think his music had the appeal that, not just Nottingham, but the country as a whole was looking for at the time. I think he got in with the right people and I think youth was on his side from the beginning and he learned his trade young.'

Zoe Kirk: 'Whenever the *Nottingham Post* have continued to write articles about Jake, and they've interviewed him many of times since, they always refer back to his first interview doing *This Is Live* with me and he acknowledges it. But it's not that well known that it was his first kind of discovery really – and that it was how his manager found him, by seeing him on my little web show. It just shows doing a small amount of publicity – even if it's local – really does help. His manager went on to find him – and look what happened!'

'Yes, it all started with *This Is Live*,' Jake told Zoe Kirk when he made a return visit to the programme the following year. 'My manager Jay saw it and got in touch. He invited me to his studio and we got on really well. Then he knew a guy who knew a guy... it went from there really.'

Jake's appearance on *This Is Live* was the start of an almost symbiotic relationship between the young singer and the *Nottingham Post*. When Bugg's career kicked in, he would begin to make regular appearances in the paper. Later those appearances would become constant. 'Every time he did something we'd interview him because we'd been starved of someone exciting to talk about,' says *EG* editor Simon Wilson. 'It wasn't like, "Haven't we done enough Jake Bugg?" Now, there's no such thing as "enough Jake Bugg".'

CHAPTER FIVE

CONFIDENT/
COCKY

Soundtrack:
Sharp Knees – 'Certain Rules' 2010
Dog Is Dead – 'Do The Right Thing' 2013
Harleighblu – 'Forget Me Not' 2013

In the autumn of 2010, Jake recorded his second session and interview, this time for commercial radio station Trent FM – not for the station's radio output, but for its podcast. The *Notts Unsigned Future Sessions* were the brainchild of Mark Del, a London-born former Nottingham University student who is one of the city's main drum-bangers when it comes to new music, and a larger-than-life character in Nottingham's music scene. 'I first saw Jake play in 2010,' Del told me. 'That's when he first started messaging me. I remember getting his messages and he was pretty confident/

cocky! But he didn't have any music. I was like, "If you don't have a track for me, there's not a lot I can do." It changed our policy. I was going, "We can't help you if you don't have a track," so we thought: Why don't we help you make a track? It was a good few months after he reached out to us that we played Jake because he didn't have a recording. We got him in for session in October 2010.'

Del had pitched a plan for the new music show – with his inbuilt evangelical zeal – to Trent's programme director at the time, Dick Stone. 'The reason behind the new music podcast – rather than putting it on air on the radio station – was that it wasn't really what the radio station was about,' Dick Stone told me. 'We were about hit music and not particularly about breaking new or unsigned artists. But we were a Nottingham radio station and I felt it was important to stay connected to that. So when Mark Del came and talked about his idea to do a show championing new music – which was very laudable at the time – it didn't really fit with what we wanted to do.'

Shaven of head and motorised of mouth, Del operated the sessions on a series of self-imposed and strictly enforced rules: Thou Shalt Only Play New Music, Thou Shalt Only Play New Music Born in the Great County of Nottingham-shire and Thou Shalt Honour and Play All Forms of New Music. The sessions were designed to give artists their first exposure – so Bugg, with the *Nottingham Post*'s *This Is Live* item already in the bag, didn't actually qualify: 'With the *Future Sessions*, you were only allowed to do one if you've never done a session before,' Del told me. 'That's the formula and the artist has to confirm that they've never done one before. I only found out recently that Jake had done a session for someone else. So he was a bit naughty – or clever, I suppose. He'd done the session for the *Nottingham Post* a month or two before. So we'll claim first radio session. He was quite proactive in reaching out to us. When he was first messaging me he was 15. It was a bit awkward. I can't go, "Let's meet down the pub and let's have a chat about it." He was 15.'

Dick Stone: 'Mark has his commandments about Thou Shalt Come from the Fair City of Nottingham and so on. Podcasts were all the rage at the time, so we thought: Why don't we do the new music angle as a podcast? So those who are interested can immerse themselves in it – binge them-selves on it – and we'll use the mainstream radio to promote it. Another branch to our tree. So that's what we did – and Jake Bugg was part and parcel of that.'

Bugg's session for *Notts Unsigned* saw him perform two songs on his sunburst Westfield guitar: the campfire country of 'Love Me The Way You Do' and the folkier 'Something Wrong'. Del introduced Bugg on the session as 'Clifton's answer to Bob Dylan', another early example of the teen-ager's name being linked to the 1960s folk singer.

At the start of the piece, Mark Del flagged up Jake as a 'potential Notts Number One of the future – fingers crossed'. To be fair, Del would say this at the start of virtually every session, regardless of who the band or singers were. Local acts like Dog Is Dead and Harleighblu have also appeared on the show. Jake – dressed in a hoodie and what seems to be the same jeans as in the *Nottingham Post* video – is so tiny that, for the opening bars of his first song, his face is completely obscured by the microphone and pop shield that he's singing into. He sings clearly and well but it lacks the deafening attack of the *Post* session. Between songs he 'chatted' with Del – Bugg's definition of chat being more succinct than most – talking about his influences, his cousin's band The Swiines and his hope for the future: 'Get famous,' is his reply, also confirming that yes, he would be happy with girls chasing him around throwing their underwear at him. It's a surprising admission for a young 'indie' musician to make.

Mark Del: 'Jake made it acceptable to succeed. With credible artists, it's not necessarily the done thing to say you want to have a Number One. If you see us interviewing him in 2010 he says he does want to have a Number One – "I want to be Number One and get rid of all that Simon Cowell pop crap." That turned out to be incredibly resonant. There'll always be people round the edges who'll be all sniffy and snooty and we don't want commercial success: "We want to play to thirty-three hairy-legged vegans because that's what gives us internal satisfaction." The definition of success for most musicians is that they can make a comfortable living. It means that they're happy. I defy any musician to look me in the eye and tell me they don't dream of making a living out of their music.'

During the *Notts Unsigned* show Jake also confirmed that he was 'halfway' through recording an album – clearly the recordings he was making with Jason Hart were bearing fruit. At that stage the plan was to release the album on Unit 24, a local indie label run on a not-for-profit basis. The label features acts like Zadkiel, Tribal Infinity and The Pittstops. 'I think Jason was involved with Jake at this stage though he didn't turn up to the session,' says Mark Del. 'In the interview Jake mentioned he was recording with someone. I believe that was at Jason's studio.'

Del was delighted with the session and saw aspects of Bugg's attitude that would come to the fore in the following years. 'The most important thing with Jake – and I think this is mostly the case with artists that are successful – is that he has the double whammy of talent and work ethic,' he told me. 'There's plenty of talented artists who are lazy and plenty of hard-working artists who sadly haven't quite got it. In my opinion, he has both and I think it is viewable in that first session. As well as talent there's distinctiveness. He has a very distinctive vocal. When you're dealing with people at the very start of their careers, you realise that there are a lot of very talented people out there... so what makes the difference? Work rate and distinctiveness are big parts of it. Existing somewhere on the planet where you can get help – are you in a scene that is very supportive or born into a family that's well connected? In Jake's case he's got the talent, he's got the distinctiveness, he's got the work rate and he happened to come along at a time when the Nottingham music scene was starting to bubble up. So from a Nottingham perspective, Jake hasn't just come out of nowhere. He's what we were hoping for. I certainly don't except him to be the last. That's what needs to happen for Nottingham to have a Manchester-type situation, in terms of a city that's recognised musically worldwide.'

By way of contrast to Mark Del's enthusiasm, for Trent FM's Dick Stone, Bugg's performance didn't really stand out. He believed that other bands that had featured on *Notts Unsigned* had a better chance of making it: 'The ones that stuck in my mind were Dog Is Dead, who then started to do well; There was Long Dead Signal, Sharp Knees… lots of different bands – and Jake was one of them. Sharp Knees did a song that really struck me. I thought: Oh, that's great. That was the one that stuck out. It wasn't the Jake Bugg session at all. Sod's Law really, isn't it? It's just one of those things. I think he caught a wave at just the right time – he was in the right place at the right time. And he hit the wave. You can't engineer it.'

Bugg's fame was still a fair way off – it would take more than a couple of webcasts for him to make it – but he clearly felt that anything other than pursuing his music wasn't a wise use of his time. He quit his music-tech course, and it's believed that Bugg did have a crack at regular employment around this time with a local heating firm. 'Let's just say they wanted me to start too early,' he later told *Shortlist* magazine. He also strayed inside one of the local chip shops he used to hang around the outside of and did a bit of work there: 'It was £20 for a three-hour shift,' he later said. 'It wasn't bad.'

Meanwhile, Bugg's incessant gigging continued into the autumn of 2010. Amongst other bookings, he played the Hockley Hustle festival. Hockley – one of Nottingham city centre's groovier areas, with a reputation for its night life and arts scene – has an annual music event, spread across various venues, that raises money for charity. Jake played at the Bodega Social Club and again earned himself a mention in *LeftLion* from reviewer Paul Klotschkow: 'It's already packed out in here by the time teenage singer-songwriter Jake Bugg takes to the stool,' Klotschkow wrote. 'He doesn't utter a word and barely makes eye contact with the crowd during his set but, when the music is this good, it doesn't matter. His songs skip along with a countryesque shuffle and there are also hints of 1950s rock'n'roll and touches of Americana in his song writing. He already sounds like a formidable talent and the scary thing is that he's still developing, so he's only going to get better.'

Things did indeed get better towards the end of 2010: Jake would get the first mainstream recognition of his music from the local BBC station in Nottingham. Schoolteacher by day and DJ by night, Dean Jackson had been on BBC Nottingham for 20 years, playing national acts as well as trying to champion local artists. He had plenty of music to play but nothing to really champion on a national level. 'The programme is called *The Beat* and it started late in 1990,' he told me. 'Local radio traditionally has been the source of new and modern music and the mission of *The Beat* back in 1990 was to start playing new music that the standard, core, local radio audience wouldn't hear elsewhere on the radio station. One of the priorities was to feature local music amongst the newer, national stuff. That's how we ended up playing Jake's mum and dad and their band, funnily enough.'

Despite trying to bang the drum for local acts, Jackson found it difficult over the years, mainly because of the perception of the Nottingham scene to outsiders: 'The frustration was growing that the Nottingham music scene was now producing music that deserved to be heard by a wider audience but the city's reputation had become... toxic is probably too strong a word to use, but you know what I mean,' says Jackson. 'Record label A&Rs weren't able to find anything to take back to their labels that was credible and marketable. I think in the end they gave up on it, so by the late nineties, probably by 2001, the music industry had kind of given up on Nottingham. Dance music-wise the city still had a very credible reputation. But in terms of guitar music on daytime Radio 1, nobody was looking at it, it was a real frustration. In those days there wasn't much I could have forwarded to Radio 1 and said, "Start playing this," because they would have said this isn't suitable for national radio, and that didn't start to change until 2008 or 2009.'

Which is where Jake Bugg comes in. 'Jake had been emailing me for a little while saying, "How do I get onto your programme?"' recalls Dean Jackson today. 'This was presumably because of this recording his mum and dad had made. And I said to him, "Until you've got something recorded, however basic, it's hard for me to know where we go with it really." But it was great to exchange emails. I did go to see him – he intrigued me and I went to see him at The Maze in Nottingham. I remember thinking: He's kind of got something. I don't think at that stage anyone knew what he'd got.'

CHAPTER SIX

TEARS ROLLING DOWN HER CHEEKS

Soundtrack:
Devendra Banhart – 'Little Yellow Spider' 2004
Jake Bugg – 'Saffron' 2010
Two Door Cinema Club – 'What You Know' 2011

Perched unprettily on a roundabout on the outskirts of Nottingham city centre, BBC Radio Nottingham is typical of many modern BBC regional centres – you might mistake it for an insurance company or medium-sized call centre if it weren't for the relatively discreet BBC logo on the side of the building. This, though, was the scene of Jake Bugg's next move towards success.

It might seem an odd place for a teenage songwriter to tout his wares. Some aspects of the station's output – like so many BBC regional stations – ploughs that slightly Alan Partridgeesque furrow of phone-ins, chat and interviews that appeals to a slightly older demographic. But one of the jobs of the BBC is to do the things that commercial stations don't or won't do. And that includes playing new, local music.

Bugg had reached out to presenter Dean Jackson – the man who'd played his parents' demo nearly 20 years earlier – prompting the DJ to check out his live act: 'I went to see Jake perform,' Jackson told me. 'I thought he was *OK*. I let him know I'd been to see him perform and, in the end, he did send in a track called "Love Me The Way You Do". Which was sent in by something called the *BBC Introducing* upload on their website.' The song, fast becoming a Bugg staple, was the same country 'twangalong' that he'd played on the Mark Del session for *Notts Unsigned*. 'I was absolutely amazed when I found the *Introducing* website,' Bugg later told Radio 1. 'I was like, "Why has no one told me about this?" I was up at two in the morning loading in tracks and the very next day Dean got back to me. I was like, "How has that just happened overnight?"'

The *BBC Introducing* connection would prove vital in the story of Bugg's rise to prominence. The *Introducing* banner covers all aspects of the Beeb's policy towards encouraging new music – and key to the process was an upload app that allowed artists to get their music to key presenters, producers and decision makers within the corporation. The BBC is a very big beast; *Introducing* was supposed to make it easier for new musicians to navigate its complex waters. It also allowed DJs from what the BBC refers to as the 'Nations and Regions' – Scotland, Wales, Northern Ireland and the various

English local areas – to feed in music from their patch. Acts from The Ting Tings to Two Door Cinema Club had all previously benefitted from *BBC Introducing* patronage. '*BBC Introducing* came along and the brief was to support unsigned, undiscovered and under-the-radar musicians,' says Dean Jackson. 'By the late 2000s there was the sense that there was music coming out of Nottingham that deserved a wider audience but, because the A&R folk had given up on it, it wasn't getting out there. The arrival of *BBC Introducing* meant I could start sending material down to London. There was a filter, obviously, in place and the producers of the new music shows in London – Radio 1 especially – would start to listen to it and they started to play Nottingham music and they had some success. Dog Is Dead were the first band that went from *BBC Introducing* to being played on daytime Radio 1 and they pre-dated Jake. Jake was the next one to come along. The role of *BBC Introducing* is key to the story really – without that, I don't think it would have ever happened.'

Dean Jackson remembers his reaction to Jake's track: 'The sound was instantly more mature than anything I'd heard or seen him do before and I remember emailing him half-jokingly saying, "Are you really 16?" And him coming back saying, "Yes, I am." I said, "Well this is brilliant." We did air that track – we played it the following Saturday. I remember the excitement – his mum got friends gathered round the radio to hear it and all the rest of it.'

Jackson's audience had what he's since described as a

'favourable' response to Jake's track. Bugg emailed him the next day thanking the DJ for playing the song – Jake Bugg: polite lad from Clifton. He asked could he come into the radio station and play Jackson some more of his material. 'By that, I took it to mean that he wanted to come in and bring a demo CD or something like that,' recalls Jackson. 'So I said, "Yes, let's sort something out." Now I can't remember the process by which this happened but that morphed from him coming in to play something off a CD to him coming into play something live on his guitar.'

By way of a warm-up for the BBC session, Jake played the night before at the Alley Cafe, a vegetarian hang-out in the city centre. He played a stinker: 'I played the worst gig ever,' Bugg later said in an interview with Radio 1. 'I think I even brought a girl – "I've got a gig so you want to come along?" I was the only person playing and three songs in, twang, string gone. No spare strings. End of gig. I said, "Sorry, folks – that's it."'

Undeterred, Jake went to the BBC the following night to play his songs but Jackson had put a proviso on Bugg coming to the studio. 'He was so young I had to insist he brought a chaperone with him,' Jackson says. 'I said you need to bring your mum, or somebody with you. He brought his cousin Grant [from The Swiines] with him as a chaperone. And that's the night he performed the session that's got "Saffron" on it.'

'Saffron' was one of three songs that Bugg performed on the BBC Nottingham session – it would later be offered as a free download on his Facebook page as a taste of things to come. He also performed 'Something Wrong' and, once again, 'Love Me The Way You Do'. 'Saffron' is a slight, finger-picking affair with a lovelorn Bugg singing to his girl – or *ger-wull*, as he pronounces it – of the title. Dean Jackson: 'As soon as Jake came and sang that, I knew instantly that we were dealing with somebody who has got the potential, who could go on to deliver. I mean, there was no question about it.'

The country folk of 'Something Wrong', a Bugg strummer with cowboy chords and mournful lyrics, is next. The session was filmed and Bugg seems a little more prepared this time – his hair looks washed and flicked and he appears to be wearing a new jumper. Jackson makes a fist of interviewing the teenager, coming up against the same problem as those who had attempted it before – that problem being that Jake Bugg doesn't care to be interviewed. 'He lacked confidence,' admits Jackson. 'In terms of the standard of the interview – it was actually probably commensurate for a 16-year-old lad, to be fair.'

Jackson did manage to squeeze a few words out of his interviewee about songwriting and his singing voice. He also elicited from Jake the story about first hearing the Don McLean song 'Vincent' on *The Simpsons*: 'The line that goes out everywhere is the line about *The Simpsons*,' says Jackson. 'He said it in that interview and it comes out in every interview he's ever done since.'

There is, however, one telling quote: when asked what his hopes are in terms of his music, Bugg replied, 'I'd love to turn it into a career. I don't have a job or anything like that. This is all I do really.'

Dean Jackson: 'Off air, I talked about his influences. Obviously I noticed the similarities with Bob Dylan but he told me that he'd never listened to any Bob Dylan. So what I was seeing there was... here was a young Bob Dylan, who hadn't heard of Bob Dylan. Do you see what I mean? It wasn't someone who was emulating Bob Dylan or being a Bob Dylan tribute. What we were seeing here was someone with all of the qualities of Bob Dylan, encapsulated in a 15/16-year-old lad and that in itself was a very enticing prospect. And it is quite hard to articulate what that special thing was but it's a sensation I've only experienced once in the 20 years I've been doing the programme. And it was on that occasion. I haven't experienced it since and hadn't experienced it before and it is slightly puzzling to think... what was it? Because actually, if you take the elements of what that performance was, in some ways it shouldn't have amounted to somebody who was going to be a musical sensation – but somehow I knew it would.'

It didn't seem to make any sense – a teenager making country-folk music that he wrote in his bedroom, deeply felt Americana from a lad who'd never been further than Mablethorpe. It went against the grain of everything else that was happening at the time. 'When he left the studio, I was aware that he could be massive,' Jackson says today. 'That sounds clichéd but it's a feeling that you rarely get with an artist you meet for the first time, let alone a teenager. I remember taking to Jules, who filmed the video, saying that something really significant has just happened there. It's difficult to pinpoint what the quality was but his voice had a tone to it that was from a very classic sixties era. But also there was something about his naivety and innocence – paired with that assured vocal – that made me think: There's something really special about this kid. For sure, what he was doing was not fashionable. In terms of marketability, in my mind I was thinking, well... there's a possibility here. Bob Dylan sold a lot of records and Donovan sold a lot of records and here's this lad, even at his tender age, who can deliver a performance almost on par with those. I remember thinking he could take the sounds of the sixties to the kids of this era – and that was the exciting thing. Because, of course, for 14, 15, 16-year-olds, they'd never heard of, or knew anything about Bob Dylan or Donovan. But the time was right for them to discover that. I just knew – it's hard to explain *how* I knew. Something happened that night and I thought: Here's someone who's blessed with the talent with the likes of Dylan – though I might be over-egging the pudding there.'

The session was a turning point as far as Jackson was concerned – and it seems that the Bugg lads agreed: as Jake and Grant left the studios, Grant Bugg told his younger cousin that he probably wouldn't have to worry about breaking strings at the Alley Café again: 'They saw the stirrings as they left the building – as we had,' says Jackson. 'Which was odd, as we hadn't discussed it. It was like,

"Thanks very much, we'll air it sometime next month." That was how it was sold to Jake.'

As 2010 was coming to an end, it's unlikely that Jake realised the stir his performance at the BBC had created. It was yet to be broadcast but the simple video of the slight young lad in the black jumper seemed to have an effect on people. No one quite knew how or why... it just did. 'A colleague of mine called Amanda Bowman was in the building presenting the late show,' recalls Dean Jackson. 'She'd met him and she was wondering what he sounded like. So I said, "Come through and have a listen." And she came through to the studio and halfway through the first track there were tears rolling down her cheek. And this was repeated – I played it to lots of colleagues and that phenomenon was repeated. I remember someone from a plugging company ringing me saying they'd seen this video that it had been playing to the office and the woman stood next to him was watching the video of him singing "Saffron" and she had tears running down her cheeks by the time she'd finished watching it.'

It was clear Jake had something – even if no one was quite sure what it was. But surely it was too old, too out of step, too steeped in the record collections of another, older generation to connect with today's rip and go young music fans. Dean Jackson says, 'We knew there was something special going on here and I remember saying, "If only the kids of today could connect with it, then something big was going to happen. That was the biggest challenge. How do you get the kids – the downloading public – to connect with somebody who's got quite an old sound?'

That concern about the way young people would react or connect with Bugg's music wasn't the initial issue: the more pressing point was getting them to hear Jake's music in the first place – then they could make up their own minds. Regional shows like Jackson's were feeding music into the central *BBC Introducing* pool to find those 'unsigned, undiscovered and under-the-radar musicians' that it was their mission statement to find. Bugg qualified on all three counts. *BBC Introducing* had decided to hold annual 'masterclasses' to bring young musicians together and help them connect with the right people in the industry – and the first one was one coming up in a matter of weeks. If Bugg was to stop being under the radar and get on it, they'd have to act quickly. Dean Jackson: 'The *BBC Introducing* masterclasses happen in the New Year and this particular year it was in Abbey Road and Maida Vale in London, and I knew Jake was a fan of The Beatles' era. So I thought it would be great for him to head to Abbey Road – so I was emailing *BBC Introducing*, pulling out all the stops to get Jake to the masterclass at Abbey Road. They don't take their instruments, it's basically two hundred musicians who go down to London. Each BBC local programme gets to put a few forward and they go down to London and they get very involved in workshops – they might talk about guitar techniques, might talk about how you get into the business and so on.'

'Since the launch of *BBC Introducing* back in 2007, we've tried to remain super clear on its specific purpose, for the BBC to support new UK musicians where we can, with unique opportunities and access to help them progress to the next stage in their own development,' says Jason Carter, the editor of *BBC Introducing*. 'This isn't necessarily about finding the next big act or success story, although if and when that happens it's an added bonus. I've managed bands in the past, before my time at the BBC, and it seemed like the Holy Grail just to get to talk to the key players in the industry – or indeed within the BBC – and to get a reply or your music listened to was invariably a pipe dream. The masterclass is the next stage in our development, an ever evolving proposition. What better places to host the day than Abbey Road and Maida Vale studios, both steeped in history? I was fortunate enough to walk into Maida Vale with one of my bands many years ago for a Peel session – we were humbled. But to be there and also hear top UK talent, leading BBC music presenters and key industry players spending time giving their own experiences to new artists – as pure as simple as that – should, if we get it right, be fantastically insightful. And the beauty of it all is, whilst only two hundred and fifty musicians can be there, all musicians from around the UK can see it all via the three online live streams and watch it on the *BBC Introducing* site any time after that. Hopefully, the *BBC Introducing* master-class is here to stay.'

When it was revealed that Jake had been successful and

had been invited to the masterclass along with 249 other hopefuls, he was bullish in an interview with BBC Nottingham: 'It feels great to be nominated,' Bugg said. 'I'm really excited. I'd love to turn music into a career. This is all I do. There's going to be some good people down there that would be good to for me to know. I would just love to make as many contacts as I possibly can.'

But the reality was that Bugg was nervous – very nervous. Dean Jackson was concerned that the quiet, inarticulate teenager might get put off by the location and the occasion and decide he wouldn't attend. Not to put too fine a point on it, Bugg might bottle it and not show up. 'We put Jake forward for this and he was accepted and had received an email telling him he could go,' Jackson recalls. 'I remember him being very nervous about it because – he's told me this since – the only time he'd left Nottingham previously was to go to Skegness or something as a kid and so he'd never been down to London. I was extremely worried he wouldn't go to this masterclass. I thought: We've spotted something that Jake's got in him and if only we can get him down to London to meet the great and the good of the record industry and radio DJs, then they might connect on the same level. Then there would be no stopping him.'

It was decided that the best thing for Jake would be a chaperone – or two – to make sure he got to London without any problems. 'The night before he rang me,' says Jackson. 'I can't remember the whole conversation but there was something about it that made me think: He's not going to go.

I couldn't go with him but I rang two guys who work on my programme, James and Juls, and asked if there was any chance they could go down to London to take part in this masterclass and take Jake with them. Which they did. They took him down there – although they did have a blowout on the M1...'

Despite this drama on the way, Jake made it to London and the *BBC Introducing* masterclass at Abbey Road on 3 February 2011 – his mum had made him some cheese-and-pickle sandwiches – and Radio 1 DJ Zane Lowe recalls chatting to Jake outside the studios. He also recalls Bugg leaving his sandwiches behind after their chat and the teenager having to slink back and collect them. 'I don't even like cheese and pickle,' Bugg later confessed. 'If it had been anywhere else, I would have just left them. But you can't fly-tip outside Abbey Road, can you?'

'Those masterclasses are great,' says Zane Lowe. 'I really like taking part in them – being in a room full of creatives and musicians – but it's very two-sided. On the one hand, everyone is there for the right reasons. On the other hand, a more awkward bunch of people you're never likely to meet in your life. I really relish the earnest awkwardness of a room like that – people who are there to just listen and learn. They're not on stage. As the musical landscape, *BBC Introducing* is incredibly important because it's a very valuable path for musicians who otherwise would have no idea how to get their music out there. It's not like you send demos to record labels anymore. *BBC Introducing* provides that avenue.'

Bugg was at Abbey Road to attend workshops, make contacts, talk to people from the industry... essentially to 'work the room'. This was not something that came naturally to him. 'There was alot of coaching between me and Jake in the meantime about what he'd take with him,' says Dean Jackson. 'I told him to take some really nice CDs with the right contact details, nicely presented, think carefully about who you're going to give those to. We spent a lot of time discussing that, how that might work, what form it might take.'

Despite not being considered one of the world's foremost meeters and greeters, Bugg seemed to come alive in the masterclass and did indeed work the room, making contacts and connections that would stand him in very good stead in the coming years: 'He found the right people and gave them CDs, including people like Zane Lowe and [BBC Radio 6 Music's] Steve Lamacq – people who would later champion him,' confirms Dean Jackson. After meeting Jake, Lamacq described him as being like 'a young Devendra Banhart from Nottingham', a rather baffling comparison as Bugg has very little in common with the hippy trippy folk singer, other than a tremulous vocal quality. Dean Jackson said, 'A couple of labels spotted him there and realised there was something about his aura... realised that there was something.'

One person who spotted Jake that day was record-company executive Mike Smith, who at the time was working for Columbia Records. 'I was looking out across the audience answering questions and my eyes rested on this one lad who was in the crowd and he looked incredible,' he says. 'He looked like a complete star, like a young Keith Richards sat there. At the end of it all I was leaving the stage and he came up and passed me a CD. People give me a stack of CDs at these events and I'll take them back to work and give them to one of the junior A&R guys to listen to. Jake's was a CD I listened to straight away and it was fantastic. It immediately showed there was genuine talent there. There was a song called "Country Song" on it. I've got to be honest, I wasn't smart enough to sign him. I really liked what he was doing but I thought it was early days. My competitors at Mercury Records immediately spotted his potential and had the guts to gamble on Jake before I did and signed him.'

Eighteen months later, Smith got a job with Mercury and ended up working with Bugg anyway: 'I got a second chance to work with somebody who is one of the biggest talents in the world right now. I think he's really going to be changing music over the next few years.'

'It was a fun day,' Bugg later said in an interview on Radio 1. 'It was mad because you're sat in a room with 200 or so other musicians – you've got guitarists looking at each other going, "I'm better than you." There was one session where we had to line up and you get thirty seconds to talk to another musician and exchange names – then the next bloke comes along and says, "All right, mate, my name's John and I'm in a punk band." Some scary looking guy. It was lovely though, a real insight – more or less like speed dating.'

It's telling that the people who met Jake that day were the

ones who would later shout his cause the loudest. One of the key mysteries to many people about Bugg's success is why people connected with songs so clearly out of step with the kind of music that was at the forefront at the time? And why did Radio 1 get behind him so wholeheartedly?

Nottingham-based music journalist Mike Atkinson: 'He received a lot of support from the BBC. I think he's the first act to hit big that's come out of *BBC Introducing* – he's *BBC Introducing*'s first star. They still play "Lighting Bolt" on Radio 1, about four or five times a week, every week to this day.'

Guitar music had lost its way; outside of metal acts, radio was finding it hard to find guitar acts that could connect with the young. Could someone like Jake be the cure? 'Radio 1 was struggling to put guitar music on their schedule at the time,' says Dean Jackson. 'Kids weren't connecting with it anymore. So here is somebody – and the significance of Jake can't be overplayed – who's taken what's become quite an old-fashioned type of music back to the kids, which is why Radio 1 are all over it. He's taken guitar music back on their playlist in a form that kids can access.'

Jake Bugg was in the right place at the right time, with the right sound and the right look. He just didn't know it yet.

CHAPTER SEVEN

GLASTONBUDGET

Soundtrack:
The Hollies – 'King Midas in Reverse' 1967
Ed Sheeran – 'You Need Me, I Don't Need You' 2009/2011
Spotlight Kid – 'Plan Comes Apart' 2011

Despite clearly making an impression on those at *BBC Introducing*, it was back to the grind of local gigs for Jake. He had gigs lined up at The Glee Club at Castle Wharf in Nottingham as well as his old stomping ground of The Maze. His gig there generated a review in *LeftLion* that seemed to catch the young singer just as he was morphing from an awkward newbie to a more rounded performer: 'He can often look like a rabbit in the headlights on stage, but tonight it looks as if he is gaining the stage presence that his songs deserve,' the review said. 'Reaching back to the fifties and sixties for songwriting inspiration; Jake Bugg sounds like Johnny Cash grappling with The Hollies, as country grapples with beat pop to create charming, heartfelt ditties. Quite rightly so, the audience is stunned into silence as they listen on intently, giving the songs the warm attention they demand.'

As well as his gigging schedule, Bugg also became a regular at the BBC Nottingham studios to see Dean Jackson: 'Jake would pop round to the BBC just for a cup of tea sometimes; he really likes the building, I think.'

The teacher turned radio presenter and the teenage musician seemed like an odd combination but the friendship lasts to this day: 'We've remained friends ever since,' Jackson told me. 'Jake's been absolutely brilliant to me and has shown tremendous loyalty and I'm extremely fond of him as a person. When he went to Number One in the album chart, I don't think he rang very many people but he picked the phone up and rang me and said, "I just wanted to say thanks," and episodes like that have happened through his life.'

There was even talk at one stage of Jackson managing Bugg: 'Briefly, yes,' confirms Jackson, 'but I said to him I wouldn't be the right person for the job. Because, although I've contacts in Nottingham, you need contacts further afield. It was a very difficult thing for me to say as I knew he was destined for greatness and I would have loved to have managed him, course I would. But there would have been a whole load of conflicts with the BBC and everything else. And although I would have loved to have managed him, it was in Jake's interest that I didn't. That was a tough thing for me to admit but, actually, that's the truth and that's been proven to be the case. Jason [Hart] manages him now. I've known Jason a long time and he's a good guy. If I had been managing him, I doubt Jake would be where he is.'

Jake would often talk with Dean Jackson about Jason Hart, who was becoming more and more involved with Bugg's life and music: 'We weren't mates,' Jackson says of the man who would become Bugg's co-manager, 'but I had interviewed him going back a long time. He had impressed me as being somebody who had his head screwed on right. So when Jake said to me, "What do you know about Jason?" I was very honest with him – well I've met him, seems a decent bloke and we've got lots of mutual friends as well who speak highly of Jason. People I trust speak very highly of him. So when Jake was running names past me, Jason was one who I thought seemed a good guy to me.'

Meanwhile, there were moves afoot involving other key players in the Nottingham music scene to give Jake a leg up to the next level. With an eye on the upcoming festival season, Bugg was about to benefit from a little behind-the-scenes planning, a touch of luck and a fairly large misunder-standing.

This next stage would involve two festivals: Nottingham's homegrown festival Splendour, and Glastonbury. Dean Jackson: 'I had nominated Jake to play at the *BBC Introducing* stage at Glastonbury. And the format for that was the same as for the *Introducing* masterclass: there's a panel in London, the good and the great, mainly from Radio 1, 6 Music, Radio 2, who decide who gets to go there and we pitch to them. I put a compelling case forward for Jake to go to the masterclass, with lots of reasons why he would be right. Having been to the masterclass, there is an affiliation with *BBC Introducing*. The next logical stage is the *Introducing* stage at Glastonbury. Now that's probably the most coveted slot that *BBC Introducing* has to offer – there aren't that many slots at Glastonbury.'

Meanwhile, Jake – always keen to get gigs under his belt – had applied for a slot at another festival: Glastonbudget. Unlike the more famous version at Michael Eavis's farm in Pilton, Somerset, Glastonbudget takes place in Wymeswold in Leicestershire, the neighbouring county to Nottingham. As the name suggests, Glastonbudget has never taken itself too seriously but it had grown considerably since it started in 2005 from featuring only tribute acts to attracting 'proper' bands like ABC and Heaven 17. Jake Bugg had spotted the festival and really fancied his chances of getting a slot. Dean Jackson: 'Jake, I hasten to add, wasn't being a tribute to anyone, they just wanted him to be himself as they did have some local talent on. He turned up to the audition and part of the judging procedure is audience reaction – and, of course, it's based on the number of people you take through the door for the judging process. I think Jake turned up with very few people. He thought: I'll go and sing and see what happens. Whereas others had gone backed by an army of fans – who had paid to get in, by the way – and the audience response, of course, was more favourable for them. Jake was very keen to play at this festival.'

But despite Jake's best efforts, the good folk of Glastonbudget said thanks... but no thanks. While this was going on,
organisers of the *BBC Introducing* stage decided to offer Jake
a slot at the real Glastonbury – a big deal and one that had an
embargo attached to it. Dean Jackson knew that the campaign
to get Bugg on the bill had been successful but wasn't allowed
to say anything. 'Jake rang me in the morning and he was a bit
deflated because he'd had the knock-back from Glastonbudget. They'd said no. And at this time he hadn't had very
many knock-backs, it had been plain sailing. One of the things
I'd said to Jake from the outset was, "Things are going a bit
too well, be prepared for the odd setback." Normally I'd say
it was one step forward, two steps back. In his case it was two
steps forward and only one step back – but even so, there'll be
the odd upset. So it was my coded way of saying something
else will come along, something better.'

Something better did indeed come along and the BBC rang
Jake to tell him the good news. Jake Bugg: 'They rang and
they said, "Do you want to play?" I was like, "Great!" I put
the phone down and thought: What just happened there? Is
somebody having me on? I rang Dean and said, "I'm playing
Glastonbudget, Dean!" And he said, "No, you're playing the
other one..."'

Dean Jackson: 'There was a silence at the end of the phone.
Jake's not the most demonstrative person – he's a very
understated character. But you could tell he was genuinely
taken aback by this news.'

Meanwhile, across town, there were other moves

underway to get Jake another festival slot – this time at Nottingham's Splendour Festival.

Bugg's trajectory through the running order of the Splendour Festival would prove to be the perfect analogy for his career: start at the bottom in 2011... and come out on top two years later. *NUSIC*'s Mark Del: 'I recommended Jake to George Akins, the promoter, to play at Splendour in 2011. He played the small Courtyard stage. In 2012 he played on the main stage. In 2013 he was headlining.'

This Is Live's Zoe Kirk was also keen for Jake to get a slot at Splendour: 'I got to choose a couple of bands that got to play and I put his name forward to the organisers and they selected him,' she says. 'They already knew about him. Straight away from my list of recommendations, they wanted him straight away. But for him to go from The Courtyard Stage, which is the smallest stage for the local bands – which is still a great stage – then two years later he's headlining Splendour Festival on the main stage is just incredible.'

The promoter of Splendour is Nottingham's Mr Music, George Akins – as well as promoting Splendour, he and his company DHP Family run venues like the Rescue Rooms, The Bodega Social Club and Nottingham's best-known venue, Rock City. Live music is part of the Akins family tradition – George's father was a music promoter before him. Very little goes on in Nottingham's music scene without George Akins being aware or involved with it – and around this time, a buzz was building about Jake Bugg. 'People were talking about him,' George Akins told me. 'There was obviously something interesting about his voice. I mean, I saw it and immediately I saw Woody Guthrie or Bob Dylan, that's what I saw straight away. I liked it – but no, I didn't recognise what was going to happen. Guy with a guitar singing songs – is it time for that? Who knows? I think all music is a rehash of something that's happened before and the only thing that makes it interesting is the voice. That's what makes it different. I think that's what Jake has – a very unique voice.'

As well as Jake's voice, Akins also believes that Bugg's moochy, slightly sullen vibe and moody attitude was also part of his early appeal – and remains so today: 'He's got a style that fitted with a lot of people from Nottingham,' Akins told me. 'That sort of Fred Perryesque, sort of football, Oasis sort of feel in his look, in his swagger, in his attitude. That's always been a very popular style of music in Nottingham and the East Midlands really – Kasabian came from nearby Leicester – so there's definitely a fashion element to Jake that's very "Nottingham".'

With two big festival slots on the horizon, Jake Bugg's trajectory seemed to be picking up speed and momentum. He even began moving up the running order of his local Nottingham acoustic shows: he was no longer bumping along on the bottom of the bill, but appearing just before the main act. In May, Jake – by now backed by a small band of local musicians – even played a gig at Nottingham's Glee Club to mark Bob Dylan's 70th birthday. He was supporting Hurray For The Riff Raff aka singer-songwriter Alynda Lee Segarra. The gig was packed and there was a sense that something was happening around the teenager – it appeared that many people were at the gig to see Jake rather than the main act. Bugg later admitted that he was genuinely nervous beforehand: 'Even my bass player – he's an experienced session player – he said he felt a bit nervous too,' he later told *This Is Live*. 'But once we got on there and the crowd were really respectful and quiet, the nerves just seemed to go away.'

Jake and his band got an encore that night – unusual for a support act – and they were offered a monthly residency at the venue for later in the year. He also managed to get a two-sentence review from the *Nottingham Post*: 'Jake Bugg and his trio opened the evening,' the review said. 'The Clifton teenager is going places – Glastonbury for starters.'

People in the Nottingham scene could sense something was happening. Gaz Peacham from The Maze, the scene of Jake's earliest gigs: 'From the first time I saw him I was like, "Wow, this guy has the potential to be something really good, he's obviously got a talent." I don't know if there was a tipping point because, even up to the last couple of times he played here, I still felt the same way. But he had improved, such a massive improvement – even though the natural talent was always there. Perhaps the tipping point was just the fact he started getting publicity outside Nottingham and obviously a few people picked him up – people like Dean Jackson started giving him a lot of publicity, local newspapers and podcasts started giving him a load of publicity and then he started getting A&R guys and management guys interested.'

On June 22, just before the Glastonbury Festival was due to start, it was decided to mark the moment with a gig/party as a send-off for the Nottingham acts heading to the festival. It would prove to be a significant night for Jake in more ways than one. 'There were a number of Nottingham bands going off to Glastonbury. One of them called Spotlight Kid had an idea of doing a Glastonbury send-off at a venue called The Bodega,' recalls Dean Jackson. 'They didn't know Jake. And they said to me, "Will you host this night?" I said I'd be honoured to host it, but obviously I need to bring the other artists that are going to Glastonbury, i.e. Jake. And so they said, "OK, Jake can open."'

In the audience at the Bodega that night was Jamie Nelson, the A&R director of Mercury Records. He'd previously worked at Parlophone Records where he'd signed the likes of Lily Allen and Eliza Doolittle. Mercury was the record label that was thinking about signing Jake after Jason Hart had passed a tape to Nelson. It would be a connection that would change his life. But for the moment, Jake was still just the opening act for the pre-Glastonbury show, alongside psychedelic shoegazers Spotlight Kid and gloom rockers Frontiers.

Dean Jackson: 'So that night, the A&R person who in the end would sign him came to that gig – I knew this guy was there and I remember getting on stage to introduce Jake, thinking: What I say here is of some significance. Normally I'd just go... Jake Bugg! But I remember standing on the stage and going to the mic and bigging up Jake. Everything I said was true but I added a bit of background, said that in my years of doing *The Beat*, artists have come and gone, but I can remember few of this age making such an impact. I suspect what you are about to witness you'll talk to the grandchildren about in decades to come. He's a very special character and, in my mind, he's destined for absolute greatness... partly knowing that in the audience was the guy who I think later that night takes him to a hotel and signs him. I don't take any credit for that but I wanted to be sure that they knew the context – that this young singer was about to take the stage – very nervously – a brilliant vocalist but not yet being able to connect with the audience. Tell them that there was something really special about him. That gig was certainly significant.'

Although he was a late addition to the bill, reviewers seemed to single Jake out as the one to watch. *BBC Introducing* reviewer Jason Dowling said, 'It may seem laughable in 2011 to tag phrases such as "incendiary" to an artist firmly entrenched in the Dylan style of songwriting but 17-year-old Jake Bugg is a rather extraordinary talent and, whilst his subject matter may have more than a hint of repetition, he has already amassed more hooks than most solo artists manage in an entire career. His voice [is] aged well beyond his years and his set, ably backed by a perfectly complementary but entirely supplementary rhythm section, offers the suggestion of something rather special, with a wealth of soaring country-rock meanderings. "Saffron" in particular shows someone who is already a master of his craft at such a tender age.

'Whether any of the night's triumvirate make significant

steps outside of the city remains to be seen but all three offer more than enough to suggest they could be at the forefront of a revival for one of the UK music scene's forgotten cities.'

Mark Del of *NUSIC* was also there that night: 'I met the A&R who signed Jake at the Glastonbury warm-up show. So in some ways, the warm-up show was more significant than Glastonbury itself. My understanding is that the A&R was a friend of Jake's manager. There were other A&Rs in the picture but Jason knew this guy, played the demo to him. He liked it. That's it. It was really that simple.'

After the warm-up came the real thing. Jake was brought onto the *BBC Introducing* stage at Glastonbury that year by Tom Robinson, BBC 6 Music presenter and a musician known for his own Dylanesque protest songs. Backed by guitar and drums – just a single snare, in fact – Jake played an eight-song set at the *BBC Introducing* stage at Glastonbury 2011 – it included old favourites, like 'Love Me The Way You Do', as well as songs that would feature on his debut album, like 'Country Song'.

It was later claimed that Robinson didn't care for Jake's attitude at the festival: 'You can take moody a bit too far,' Robinson is reported to have said. 'The only one who scowled all the way through, didn't exchange a friendly word with anybody, was Jake Bugg. Good luck to him with his music but you can at least be nice to people, for goodness' sake!'

'He said how I was being the moody one and didn't come and say "Hi" to him but he was the one looking like he was the don,' Jake later said when he was asked about the incident by Nottingham journalist Simon Wilson. 'I didn't want to go say hello to him because he looked like he wouldn't appreciate it. If anyone speaks to me, I'm sound with them.'

Bugg added – in the kind of backhanded comment that would soon be annoying boy-band members: 'If there's one person who is going to dislike you, I'd rather it be Tom Robinson than someone like Zane Lowe.'

Other acts that year to appear on the *Introducing* stage included Crow Black Children, Sharks Took The Rest and D/R/U/G/S. Much of the attention that year was focused on Ed Sheeran but the *BBC Introducing* blog site also predicted big things for Jake: 'Such a strong distinctive voice, simple guitar-picking melodies, and lyrics that make it hard to believe this young singer-songwriter from Nottingham is only 17. After seeing him play at Glastonbury, it was clear he was producing music way beyond his years, but it was his whole manner that was mature. With only a handful of words between songs, and barely raising a smile, you might have thought he was shy or nervous, but it didn't feel that way at all in his presence. He seemed to command the stage with such confidence and purpose, without feeling the need to babble on about nonsense between songs, but to just let his songs do the talking, one by one. Being influenced by the likes of Donovan, Don McLean, Bob Dylan, The Beatles, and Jimi Hendrix, you could say Jake was born in the wrong era, but we need these kinds of songwriters here with us now in 2011 and beyond, carrying the torch and keeping the spirit of Dylan and co. alive. He certainly has time on his side, and who knows how far this boy can go.'

Dean Jackson believes that Glastonbury was a turning point – for Jake and for him. 'I wasn't at Glastonbury that day, I wasn't there,' Jackson told me. 'In some ways Glastonbury was a release for me – it was the place promoter I wanted to get Jake to really. There were two things: I was convinced we had to get him to the *BBC Introducing* masterclass in London. I don't know why, I don't know the rationale behind it, it was a gut feeling, but I knew we had to get him there for some reason. The second phase was to get him to the acoustic stage at Glastonbury. I knew/imagined that if I got him there, everything would be fine. From that point onwards, it was handed over to whoever was looking after him. My part was done and by this point Jason [Hart] his manager was on the scene, so it was a relief for me really. It was a relief that it went well.'

While he was there Jake tried his hand at a little Glastonbury camping – to sample the full festival experience – then he returned to Nottingham. It had been a learning experience – chiefly because, if he learned anything, it was that he never wanted to endure the full Glastonbury experience again. 2011 would be the one and only time he would attempt festival camping – he vowed never to do it again. 'I hated it because there was so much mud and I didn't take any wellies,' he later said.

Back in Nottingham, it was time for Splendour. The headliners that year were camp disco-ologists Scissor Sisters – much further down the bill on The Courtyard Stage, sponsored by *LeftLion*, was Jake Bugg. Splendour promoter

George Akins says the Jake Bugg he saw that day was a very nervous character and those nerves had a direct effect on his performance: 'He had a 30-minute set but his songs were so short and he did it so quickly – I think it was 15 or 20 minutes he did – and then he was off,' Akins told me. 'I was like, "What are you doing? You've got a half-hour set." I think he must have been quite nervous doing a show like that.'

Despite – or maybe because of – Jake's nervous energy, he still managed to generate a short but positive review in the *Nottingham Post*: 'Jake Bugg, fresh from his set at Glastonbury, opened The Courtyard Stage, his quivering John Denver-like voice working well in the intimate setting.'

George Akins: 'That was so early in his progression – he would have been about 17. The performance I saw on The Courtyard Stage in 2011, compared to the performance I saw in 2013 on the headline stage... light years apart. There's no doubt that there's been a real strive in Nottingham to push him forward and champion him. Getting his Glastonbury *Introducing* spot, which came through Dean Jackson, was a key moment for Jake; getting Jason Hart noticing him was another key moment; doing Splendour... key moments.'

Behind the scenes another key moment had taken place – the news of Jake's record deal was about to break. Nottingham was about to become the focus of attention as a musical city for the first time since Paper Lace stepped out onto the balcony of Nottingham Town Hall back in the 1970s. For years, Nottingham had been in the backwater – now it was about to take its place firmly in the spotlight.

CHAPTER EIGHT

WE ALL GET LAID

Soundtrack:
Wiz Khalifa – 'Rolling Papers' 2011
Ronika – 'Automatic' 2012
The Vamps – 'Can We Dance' 2013

When the news about Jake's deal with Mercury Records broke, it seemed to cement a feeling that Nottingham's moment was tantalisingly close. Maybe it had even arrived. With Jake's rise – and that of other local acts – could the days of novelty records and one-hit wonders finally be put to rest?

Mercury Records is a label that has gone through many phases and styles since it first appeared in 1945. From jazz through heavy metal, goth and country and western, Mercury has been there, seen it, done it. The label's current roster of talent is an eclectic mix to say the least – very much like Jake Bugg's music – of old and new. The late Johnny Cash is there alongside ex-Beatle Paul McCartney... dance act Chase and Status rub shoulders with teen pop-soul act The Vamps.

When he was signed, Bugg was swimming against the tide of where the good money was being bet – maybe that ultimately worked in his favour... maybe it was time for a change. 2011 was the year of female artists like Rihanna, Adele and Jessie J – occasionally, the women would allow a male artist to occupy the top of the charts, like Bruno Mars or Professor Green. Countryfied rockabilly-folk along the lines that Jake Bugg was touting was in short supply. 'The pop market got saturated with that ghastly R&B club-banger thing,' says Nottingham-based music journalist Mike Atkinson, who would play a vital part in pushing Jake onto the national stage. 'I enjoyed it for a while, some of that David Guetta early stuff, but I think Rihanna seized it, ran with it and ran it into the ground. So I think Jake was a reaction against the complete saturation of that one particular genre in the charts for a couple of years. It represents the fact that there are a lot of people in their teens reaching back to a... bolder, more classic song style, so it's a representation of their tastes. They've found their own paths to this music. It's to do with the fact that the past is now the present and everything is equally available. The gatekeepers – like music journalists – don't matter as much and people are just finding their own way through to the music that they love and it's kind of disassociated itself from notions of generation or whatever.'

BBC presenter Dean Jackson has his own take on why the time was right for Jake: 'Bugg looked like the kids and talked like the kids and that was enough for them to accept his sound. He was communicating stories about their lives – the style of music would be accepted if the message and the style could be related to. He was like a rapper – only he didn't rap. Country and western songs were never going to connect with kids – we know that. But Jake was edgy and I knew the sort of life he'd lived, I knew he was bringing that out in his lyrics – so he's got the kind of lyricism of a rapper in many ways. I'd already had hints of him using quite urban language in his songs. His experiences were everything you expected a rapper to have. He wasn't a tribute artist, he wasn't emulating somebody else – he'd come up with all of this in the structure of his songs, in what he was doing musically. When he'd name-checked some of the big names beforehand, what Jake was doing was unique. And so I think, in terms of what he was doing musically and in terms of his lyrics, clearly he'd got the ability to connect with a young audience and to take guitar music back to them.'

'From the heart of Nottingham comes the precociously talented Jake Bugg,' was how Mercury Records put it. 'Discovering music through a Don McLean song he heard whilst watching *The Simpsons*, his is a very modern folk tale. With a musical diet consisting of Dylan, Glen

Campbell, Wiz Khalifa and more, it's as eclectic as it is unique. Newly signed to Mercury, his tales of growing up and friendship, sharply observed, are set to make him the troubadour to watch in 2012.'

With Jake's Mercury deal now common knowledge in Nottingham, this wasn't the moment for coy congratulations – Mark Del's NUSIC site covered the news with undisguised glee, sniffing the possibility that a much sought Number One could be one step closer: 'Jake Bugg has become the third Nottinghamshire artist to sign a major label record deal in the last six months!!' the site proclaimed. 'Following in the footsteps of Dog Is Dead and (we believe) Natalie Duncan, it's incredibly exciting to see the London-based music industry finally cottoning on to the huge amount of talent in the Great County of Nottinghamshire, and we are sure these three will not be the last! [Singer, songwriter and DJ] Ronika, for example, must be attracting major-label interest after featuring in this week's NME (AGAIN). Jake has signed to Mercury Records, they are owned by Universal who are the world's biggest record label, this is big-time news. We're talking the home of Chase and Status, Arcade Fire and some band called U2. Yes, our lad is roster buddies with the world's biggest band! Good luck, Jake, we can't wait to hear that Number One album!'

Jake marked the news of his signing with a return to the Nottingham Post's This Is Live podcast and gave Zoe Kirk his take on what had happened since he'd had his first exposure a year earlier: 'It's very strange, yeah,' he told her, looking and sounding a little more polished than he had almost exactly 12 months ago. 'I never thought I'd get so far, to be honest. It's all very mad.' Kirk also asked him about his plans to release records: 'It's just about keeping the momentum and keeping it real. It's not about making it a big artificial thing – keeping it natural and raw.'

A lot had changed over the space of a year. According to Zoe Kirk, 'He came back a year later to do *This Is Live* again – he'd just signed to Mercury. His manager Jay got back in touch and said could he come on again – and I said, "Of course, absolutely."' Kirk found that Bugg was a little more forthcoming than the tongue-tied 16-year-old she'd met 12 months earlier. 'He'd got a bit more to say this time – he was a different chap. He still hadn't done that many interviews but he was a bit more confident; he was a bit older, I guess. It was funny hearing him chat about just signing to Mercury.'

Signing the deal changed perceptions of Bugg in his home city. In Nottingham, Jake ceased to be merely 'Jake Bugg'; he became 'newly signed to Mercury Records Jake Bugg'. The city itself was beginning to appear on the national musical radar and Jake was about to get his first mention in a national newspaper. On 29 September 2011 music journalist Mike Atkinson wrote a piece for *The Guardian* under the headline: NOTTINGHAM'S MUSIC SCENE: SOON TO BE HEARD. In it, Atkinson laid out a case for Nottingham coming to terms with its musical past and staking a claim to being a genuine musical force in the future. Atkinson explained to me the background to the piece, 'The line I took, that the music scene was crap and now it's great, was the line I had to take in my pitch in order to get the pitch accepted. I know what sort of stories Michael Hann [associate music editor of *The Guardian*] would go for. If I went in for an article saying, "Oh, there are lots of good musicians in Nottingham, let's write an article on them," he'd go, "Well, you can say that equally about any town – there are good musicians in every town. What's the story?" What made it a story was the fact that we have historically underachieved, not in terms of musical quality, but underachieved terms of getting wider recognition for Nottingham music. And we seemed to reach a moment in 2011 where that was suddenly changing – a new generation were coming through and I knew that would be the hook that would frame the piece and that would be the hook for getting people to read the article.'

Atkinson – who lives in Nottingham but rarely had the opportunity to write about the city's music scene – got the go-ahead for the piece.

But the focus of the article wasn't Jake Bugg – he was something of an afterthought. Atkinson went on, 'At the time when I pitched it, there were only three artists I was going to write about, which were Liam Bailey, Dog Is Dead and Ronika. Liam Bailey already had a Top Five with Chase and Status, so he was up and running; Ronika was getting a lot of critical respect and blog love for her second single, which had already been mentioned in *The Guardian*, in fact, and I was aware she was building a national following. And Dog Is Dead had just signed the deal.'

Dog Is Dead were very much the focus of the article. The band – managed by Nottingham promoter and venue owner George Akins – had formed at school in the West Bridgford area of Nottingham and had also been championed by *BBC Introducing*. 'I came across Dog Is Dead when they were supporting another band at The Bodega Social,' Akins told me. 'One of the managers said, "There's a local band on, apparently they're really good, they've brought two hundred friends down." "Oh, I'll come down and check them out." So I went to see them, they were amazing, went to see them at Junction 7, which is a small bar at the top of the road, and we took them on and managed them. It was difficult at the time – Nottingham was not on the radar for record companies or anyone in that sense. It was almost like nothing comes out of Nottingham, because there's nothing in there.'

Dog Is Dead had been signed to Atlantic Records earlier in 2011 and had appeared in an episode of TV show *Skins*. Every indication was that the Dogs, with their spacey, disco pop, were about to have their day. There was, in Atkinson's view, a weight of expectation on Dog Is Dead's shoulders. 'I don't think there's that kind of pressure,' the band's lead singer Rob Milton said in the article, 'because we've had all the support we need. So it spurs us on, in a way. It's something to be proud of and, in fact, it helps us nationally – because it's more interesting, coming from a place without anything. Coming back to Nottingham after two months on tour, you notice that there [are] three or four artists who are pushing to a stage where we were a few months back. It's happened really quickly and it hasn't really happened before.'

Other up-and-coming local acts that were name-checked in the piece were Nina Smith ('understated acoustic pop'), Kirk Spencer ('Indian-influenced electronica') and Swimming ('synthy, cosmic indie-rock'). And Jake Bugg.

Mike Atkinson had been at Splendour in 2011 when Bugg was bottom of the bill at The Courtyard Stage. 'Jake Bugg only came on my radar halfway through researching the piece,' Atkinson now admits. 'At the Splendour Festival in 2011, I went down to interview Dog Is Dead – and because there were a lot of Nottingham acts on the bill and I wanted to check them out. Jake was bottom of the bill on the *Leftlion* Courtyard stage, he was the first guy on stage on the day. I didn't even bother going to look at him – I'd never heard of him. I thought: Well, you can't watch everyone, there was no interest there, so I completely missed that! I then caught him at the Y Not Festival at Matlock in Derbyshire, where Dean Jackson had a *BBC Introducing* stage. By that time, I *had* heard of him and thought I'd better check him out. I was really knocked out by his set – I thought it was really, really impressive. At first I was a bit, "There's that bloke with the reedy voice that I don't quite get." At the end of the half-hour set, I thought: God, this guy is really good.'

Jake's inclusion in *The Guardian* article reads like the afterthought it essentially was: 'Nottingham's newest significant arrival is 17-year-old Jake Bugg, a plaintive performer with a distinctive, reedy voice and a knack for writing songs that already sound decades old. Bugg, who signed to Mercury over the summer, is a beneficiary of the *BBC Introducing* initiative, which aims to support "unsigned, undiscovered and under-the-radar" musicians. Its website provides an upload facility for new acts, who can tag their tracks by genre and region. Any submissions from the East Midlands are automatically routed to Dean Jackson, a music presenter at BBC Radio Nottingham. Jackson and his team typically receive around 200 tracks a week. They aim to listen to at least 95 per cent. The dream conclusion of this process is a place on the Radio 1 playlist, which reserves a weekly slot for *BBC Introducing* acts. This year, four tracks from Nottingham acts have qualified for inclusion, including Jake Bugg's "Someone Told Me" and "Young" by Dog Is Dead, a dextrous and characterful five-piece who have since signed to Atlantic.'

'It was Jake's first mention in the national press in that article,' Atkinson says today, telling me that, of all the pieces he's ever written, this one was to have to most impact. 'When I wrote it I wasn't really thinking about the people of Nottingham or the people at *The Guardian*, I was thinking about what would be of wider interest to the readers of the paper. If it just said there were great things in Nottingham, people would just say, "I don't care – I don't live in Nottingham." But I thought it would be interesting to examine the reasons why things had started to change in Nottingham. I thought that people in other cities could maybe learn from the example of those in the Nottingham scene. So I widened it out a bit and talked about how people now use social media, talked about the impact of *BBC Introducing*. I hadn't really been involved in the Nottingham scene much before that. I'd done the odd thing on the odd person, but I shared the general perception that there was nothing interesting going on here, just a bunch of local bands, with all the stigma that comes with being a local band. So when I found the initial three acts I thought: Oh, there's three acts worth writing about. But it wasn't until I started researching the piece that I realised that they were just the tip of a vast iceberg of talent.'

Some members of Nottingham's vast iceberg of talent weren't too happy when Atkinson's article appeared. There was a fair amount of grumbling, particularly among those who hadn't been name-checked. This was something that *NUSIC*'s Mark Del became acutely aware of. The ever positive Del attempted to smooth things over... in his own inimitable way: 'When *The Guardian* article came out there was a lot of... errr, where's my band? Why wasn't I in that article? My analogy was not my usual football one, but a sex one. Imagine that Nottingham University puts out some research that proves that all men from Nottingham are better in bed and they use me, Mark Del, as the example. All the other men in Nottingham can get their egos in a twist and go, "How come they're talking about how great Mark Del is in bed?" Or they focus on the bigger positive, which is: we're all going to get laid. The benefit is for the greater good. There are individuals that the focus naturally lies on but look at the greater good. We all get laid.'

Meanwhile, a new name came into the frame as part of Team Bugg: Keith Armstrong. Though Jason Hart can very much take the credit for getting Jake to this stage, it would be Armstrong's experience that helped get him to the next. Here was a man behind many of the kind of records that Jake's parents would have loved in the 1980s. Armstrong started the Kitchenware record label in 1982 when he was a 21-year-old manager of an HMV store in Newcastle. The label was responsible for the swoonsome pop stylings of Prefab Sprout, the electronic soul of Kane Gang and later the *sturm und drang* doom rock of Editors. Kitchenware took over management of soft-pop mega-sellers The Lighthouse Family, best known for their hit 'Lifted'. The band, despite being resolutely unfashionable with critics, sold ten million records worldwide. It was via Jason Hart's musical connection with ex-Lighthouse Family man Paul Tucker in their short-lived band The Orange Lights that he made the connection with Armstrong. Before long, the musical entrepreneur would eventually close down Kitchenware and concentrate his management skills solely on Bugg via a new management and publishing company called Soul Kitchen Music & Management – Jake was to be the first signing.

'Jake comes from the largest council estate in Europe and he's taught himself how to play the guitar and sing,' Armstrong would later explain to the *Newcastle Journal*, describing what it was that appealed to him about the teenager. 'He's the classic "get out of the ghetto" inspiration story and I'm sure he's destined for massive things. For a while it hasn't been as easy for musicians to make it because there's so much focus on these talent shows like *X Factor*. There are a lot of really talented people out there looking for a break and I want to empower those people and help them do well.'

Or, as Bugg himself put it, 'I got lucky. I met a guy in Nottingham who knew a guy in Newcastle who knew a guy down in London who works for a record label. Six months later, I was signed.'

For Jake himself, there was still plenty of work to be done. He'd started a residency at Nottingham's Glee Club – playing once a month – and also started racking up some heavyweight support slots... and some unlikely ones too, such as opening for dance act Example at Rock City. Mark Del: 'Part of Jake's story is working hard, touring hard, playing gigs, doing some big support slots and doing some random ones too. He supported Example, for example. I remember thinking: What? That is so random. But it got him in front of a big audience. Those prominent Jake support slots are definitely part of the story.'

The end-of-year round-up for 2011 in the entertainment pages of the *Nottingham Post* had plenty to shout about in terms of local talent – and especially that of Jake Bugg: 'The 17-year-old from Clifton was another major-label signing for Nottingham this year, snapped up by Mercury Records, who flew him to Nashville last month to record his first single for the label. His track "Someone Told Me" was playlisted on Radio 1, he was at Glastonbury for *BBC Introducing* and last week he opened for Example at his sold out Rock City show. Despite a consistently rich local music scene, chart success has been, to say the least, disappointing. You have to go back decades to find the last time a home grown band or singer made any impact on a national or international scale. And even then it's hardly credible: Su Pollard, Paper Lace, erm, Alvin Stardust. It's perhaps only sixties blues rockers Ten Years After who you'd really want to shout about. There have been others but the connections to the city start to hang by a thin thread. Stereo MCs moved to London before they were Stereo MCs. Ditto Tindersticks. And yes, there was that bloke from Air Supply... it's hardly Manchester. But this year has seen a real change in the fortunes of our music scene.'

Nottingham's favourite drum banger Mark Del seized the moment to make what seemed like a rash prediction: 'With Dog Is Dead, Jack Bugg, Natalie Duncan and [singer-songwriter] Shide Boss all signed to majors, I predict at least one Top Ten album and maybe even that hallowed Number One. There is a lot of talent in the colleges and cul-de-sacs of suburban Notts. 2012 will quite simply be the most incredible year of all time for the Nottingham music scene. Sorry about sitting on the fence there.'

Back home in Clifton, Jake would receive perhaps the ultimate local accolade on the run-up to Christmas: 'The switch-on of Clifton Christmas lights on Friday will include live music and a Santa's grotto,' reported the *Nottingham Post*. 'Santa will be at the library in Southchurch Drive from 2pm to 4.30pm. There will be a £1 entry fee and all children will receive a present. Choirs from Milford and Dovecote primary schools will be performing carols. Local singer-songwriter Jake Bugg, who performed at Glastonbury Festival, a Clifton street-dancing group called Dancing Motion and Farnborough School Choir will hit the stage in the car park of The Peacock pub from 5pm to 7pm.'

It would be quite a while until Jake would spend much quality time in Clifton. The gigs he'd play would be considerably bigger than the car park of The Peacock pub – his career was about to take off and his music was going to take him around the world.

CHAPTER NINE

JIMMY CLIFF SHOOK MY HAND

Soundtrack:
Johnny Cash - 'Folsom Prison Blues' 1955
Snow Patrol – 'Run' 2004
Michael Kiwanuka – 'Home Again' 2012

It is quite a leap but it seems to symbolise the way Jake Bugg's life and circumstances changed as 2010 turned into 2011. In December 2010 he was playing in the car park of The Peacock in Nottingham for the Christmas lights switch-on. A few weeks later he was appearing on BBC2's highbrow *Review Show*, performing a song that would become his first single: 'Trouble Town'.

Watched by actress Maureen Lipman and actor David Morrissey – Bugg had to ask manager Jay Hart who they were – he played the song as a straight acoustic affair at the end of the show. In a move reminiscent of the time he played his first Splendour set and got told off for finishing too quickly, he battered through 'Trouble Town' so swiftly he managed to beat the end credits of the programme. This left an uncomfortable, silent gap before the show ended. 'It's about growing up in Clifton,' Jake told the *Nottingham Post*. 'But it's also about any other council estate,' he added. This would be typical of the diplomacy Bugg would have to learn when discussing his 'Clifton songs'. None were what you'd call complimentary about the area he grew up in. 'People do want to get out of those places and travel the world or live the dream. It's not just Clifton. I recorded the video for it in Clifton with a few of my mates and some of my cousins. When you're growing up, you want to get away. I think that's a feeling that everyone's experienced as a teenager. You want to go out, travel the world, see things for yourself. And luckily, I'm doing that through my music.'

The retro, super-8 tinged video for 'Trouble Town' was shot by Nottingham filmmaker Michael Holyk, a self-taught director who made his first video at college and got a BBC traineeship aged 17. Despite being a Nottingham lad, he had to bid for the job like everyone else: 'No artist communication,' he told *LeftLion*, describing the process of getting a video commission. 'You simply get something in your inbox and you pitch for it. I do a ten-page document. If they like it, good. If they don't, they'll just say no. The higher up you get, the more detached you are from the artist. There's a Notts connection and I was fortunate enough to know his management. That's another thing: you can do the best pitch in the world but if you're friendly with the artist's management or you've got a good name, they'll work with you. It's really bad and it shouldn't be like that but it is. Persistence is the key; you keep banging them out and going for it and sooner or later they'll go with one of your ideas.'

The song's lyrics, with its talk of tower blocks, kids being chased by cops, smoking cheap weed and getting by on benefits, laid out an effective case for his 'council estate Dylan' tag in less than three minutes. Nice and short – just like singles used to be in the old days.

The song was produced by seasoned musician Iain Archer – who had a novel approach to getting the take used as Bugg's debut, as Jake explains: 'I was in the studio with Iain and he left a microphone on by accident and it was just that *sound*. We sent it to the label and they said, "Great, we want to put it out as a record." I was the one saying, "No, I want to record it again."'

But it wasn't Archer's production that caused ripples in muso circles – it was his co-writing credit. Archer, from Bangor in Northern Ireland, is probably best known as being a songwriter and sometime guitarist with polite rockers Snow Patrol. The band, led by Gary Lightbody, had been plucky but largely unsuccessful indie sluggers until their 2002 album *Final Straw*. Archer had come on board as a touring guitarist but had a hand in writing several tracks on the album, which saw Snow Patrol finally get the commercial success they had been striving for. One song in particular struck a chord – a lighters-in-the-air anthem called 'Run'.

It had been Jake's now co-manager Keith Armstrong who had the idea to team Bugg with Archer: 'Jake's management team are well connected to the people who music publish me,' Archer told *MusicWebNews* in 2013. 'It's an interesting thing – there are certain people in the music business who are very, very intuitive and can spot characters who'll work together, and I think that's a real gift that some people have. They thought: We should really try to team Jake and Iain up, those guys could be an interesting match and, from the moment Jake came into my studio and we started working together, it was catalytic. We immediately started to hatch musical plans and [come] up with lots of exciting pieces of music.'

Archer's reputation was as a backroom boy, despite releasing three solo albums in the noughties; he was happy to stand in the shadows: 'It's music that excites me, not notoriety. Creating good work and lasting music. I feel extremely fortunate to be in the position where I can get up every day and go to the studio and make records. Wow. It blows my mind. I have a studio in the bell tower of an old church in North London. I climb some stone steps, get away from the world and make music. It's beautiful. That's where we recorded a lot of Jake's record.'

Other tracks were recorded further north in Liverpool at the Motor Museum, a studio in the city's buzzing Lark Lane area. The tracks that featured a full band were mainly done at the studios, which are run by Orchestral Manoeuvres in the Dark (OMD) front man Andy McCluskey, surely a favourite of Jake's 1980s-pop loving parents. There was a 'bang it down' attitude towards recording and one track was even pulled straight from a recording made on Jake's iPhone. Whatever the recording environment or equipment, the aim was for a live sound: 'Yeah, man, all of it was live, that's the way I like to do things,' Jake later told journalist Rob Power. 'Except a couple of them, like "Taste It", "Trouble Town" and "Lightning Bolt", they were demos, and "Broken" was a demo as well. We didn't even try recording them again. The record label thought they sounded great, so I was happy that I didn't have to do it again! All the rest of them are live. I definitely wanted that kind of sound but I also wanted it to sound slightly contemporary, to have a contemporary twist to it. And I just wanted to mix things up a bit, see what happened. I'm very happy with it to be honest.'

This new idea of Jake sharing songwriting credits with older, more seasoned musicians, would see him come in for criticism in some quarters – to some, it seemed to undermine his much vaunted authenticity. It also saw a shift from the more plaintive, acoustic numbers he had been performing in Nottingham to rockier propositions like 'Trouble Town'. 'I certainly had those thoughts,' admits music writer Mike Atkinson. 'I dialled back on him a bit after that. "Trouble Town" has that demo quality – I think he bashed that out quite quickly and they thought: We'll bung that out. I'm sure there was some gentle encouragement for him to do more in that vein. I can't speculate on the role Iain Archer has played creatively. I'd like to think Jake was going to head down that direction anyway but he got encouraged to do so. I think it's a mixture. I've never been a Snow Patrol fan.'

BBC Nottingham presenter Dean Jackson believes involving other songwriters at this stage was a logical move: 'I think that, when you've got an artist Jake's age – remember that when he was signed, he was only 17 – and he'd got lots he wanted to say, the logical thing to do is give him a mentor. There's nothing unusual in that and I think it's the right thing to do. I don't have a problem with that – it's gone on since time immemorial. Co-writing is interesting and, to me, these people are mentoring his craft, they're not people who are brought in because Jake can't write – and I think it's important for that distinction to be made, because we know that he can write. And for a 17-year-old to be told, "Right, we need an album in three or four months," without providing that framework – I think would be disastrous for all concerned.'

The issue that became something of a thorn in Bugg's side was, if you're so authentic, why involve others? 'The people I've written with are mates of mine,' Bugg said when asked about the co-writing issue in an interview with *Shortlist*. 'You have a cup of tea, sit down with a couple of guitars and make a tune. If you look back through time, people have always written songs together. And you learn things that you wouldn't if you were writing on your own. Some people will have a piece of music put in front of them and they'll just sing it. They don't care what they're singing.'

NUSIC's Mark Del believes that outside a certain muso circle, the songwriting question isn't an issue and, like Dean Jackson, is quick to jump to Bugg's defence: 'Most people don't know,' he says. 'I think that's a trainspottery thing. I don't think many of the million-odd people who bought his debut album across the world have looked at it and gone, "Oh my God... Iain Archer's on half of these songs!" I don't think that happens. I don't think people are that bothered about it. I don't think I've ever heard one fan even mention it. Only the odd muso. You've got to remember his age. He's learning the craft of songwriting. I don't think it would bother Jake either. He's such a laid-back guy.'

Jake himself – clearly getting better at the whole 'being interviewed' thing – would later come up with a fairly outrageous soundbite to fend off the criticism that sharing songwriting credits would generate: 'Sometimes Lennon needed McCartney and sometimes Simon needed Garfunkel,' he told *The Guardian*. 'You'd go mad doing everything on your own.'

Although 'Trouble Town' didn't chart – despite big backing from Zane Lowe, the Radio 1 DJ Jake had met at *BBC Introducing* over a cheese-and-pickle sandwich – it started a buzz about the young singer. It was a buzz that would increase after 'Country Song', a track that Jake wrote in his bedroom back in Clifton, was used on a TV advert for beer. Jake, who had only just turned 18 when the advert was released, appears in voice only, singing his lament to greener times and a desire to look beyond places like Clifton, even if it's only in your mind. The advert – created by advertising agency Grey London for Greene King IPA – was set in a North London pub called The Hornsey Tavern, and its slow-motion images of friendliness and 'ideal pubiness' were designed to appeal to younger drinkers of a distinctly old-fashioned drink: India pale ale. Under the strapline 'Crafted For The Moment', the ad was debuted during the FA Cup semi-final on ITV in April. For a new artist to hook up with a multi-million pound brand relaunch was a massive coup. For the advertisers, it looked like a canny move: Bugg was young yet of another time, just the look they were going for. Early Bugg supporter Gaz Peacham adds, 'I vividly remember the first time I saw the Greene King advert with Jake on. I remember sitting there and watching it and I turned to my other half and went, "That's Jake Bugg's voice," and she went, "Yeah, it sounds like him, doesn't it?" We Googled it and we were like, "That's Jake Bugg's song! No way, he's on the Greene King advert! That's going to give him some exposure!"'

The Bugg buzz would increase even further after Jake appeared on Jools Holland's *Later* show on BBC2 a few weeks later. A booking on *Later* was usually a strong indicator that a new artist was about to break through. It was a path that the likes of Ed Sheeran and Emeli Sandé had both recently taken to great effect. The episodes of *Later* and *Later Live* that Bugg appeared on – which featured live and pre-recorded versions – were a typical mix of the old and the new, the mainstream and the left field, the low key and the raucous. This was ideal territory to showcase someone like Jake Bugg. Reggae legend Jimmy Cliff was there along with maniacal Swedish rockers The Hives and English chanteuse Paloma Faith. 'It was cool, man,' Bugg later told the *Nottingham Post*. 'It was bang on. To watch it on TV and then actually be there on it was crazy. Jimmy Cliff came over after and shook my hand. (Bugg later confessed he didn't know who the "Harder They Come" singer was prior to the appearance.) Paloma Faith looked after me because I was a bit nervous. Well, I was the new boy. And we had a couple of technical faults on the pre-record. There was feedback on the first song so we had to do it again. It made us look a bit silly because we had to follow Jimmy Cliff. And then the mic stopped working on the second one. I was more relaxed about the live show than the pre-record. It was crazy because Jimmy Cliff was watching as I was performing. That was a strange experience. But he and Paloma Faith came over after and said they thought it was good, which was great.'

Bugg played 'Country Song' in a style that his Nottingham followers would recognise – just him with an acoustic. But when he played new song 'Lightning Bolt', it was a very different proposition. He had a younger band, a Liam Gallagheresque buttoned-up jacket and an electric guitar rather than an acoustic. In fact, the guitar was a smart new Fender Telecaster: 'For his 18th I bought him a Fender Telecaster,' Jake's dad David told journalist Simon Wilson. 'It was such a proud moment to see him playing that on stage and on TV.'

This new, amped-up version of Jake Bugg took some people by surprise. *Guardian* music journalist Mike Atkinson said, 'If he was still the act that he was when I saw him live in summer 2011, I would have been gobsmacked that he would have become an international superstar. He had a different backing band with him then, two much older guys. What changed? I think he started broadening his musical reach after signing to Mercury. "Trouble Town" was totally different from anything anyone had heard him play. There were no rockers in his set two years ago, it was always like "Someone Told Me" and "Country Song". The game changer was "Lightning Bolt". I mean, the very first time I heard "Lightning Bolt", I thought: Fuck, he's just come on in leaps and bounds here, this is a really, really great track. It was only after hearing "Lightning Bolt" that I began to see him as a serious contender for future greatness, as it were.'

'I thought I needed something to compliment the more melancholic side of what I do,' Jake told *Face Culture*, when asked about these more up-tempo tracks. 'I thought I'd write a few faster ones. Iain had a few chords, I sang a little country melody... just messing around. And we wrote "Lightning Bolt". It took us five minutes. Mental.'

After the Jools Holland appearance, Jake Bugg's name trended on Twitter, with the likes of Lily Allen and Radio 1's Fearne Cotton voicing their approval. 'Country Song' – all 1 minute, 45 seconds of it – was released as a single. Produced by Jason Hart and with Bugg credited as the sole songwriter, it only made it to Number 100 in the charts. A black-and-

Jake backstage at the
Splendour festival in
Nottingham 2012 – he
went from bottom of the
bill to headliner in the
space of three years.
© Getty Images

Left: Jake's first ever photo shoot in 2010, on the set of *This Is Live*.

Courtesy of Nottingham Post

Right: Zoe Kirk, presenter of *This Is Live*, the web show that gave Jake his first break.

Courtesy of Nottingham Post

Left: One of Jake's earliest supporters, Dean Jackson of BBC Nottingham.

Courtesy of Juls Chambon

Left: Jake in 2012, shortly after the release of his debut single 'Trouble Town'.

© *Rex Features*

Right: A more assured looking Jake in 2011, making his return to *This Is Live* after getting a record deal.

Courtesy of Nottingham Post

Left: Outspoken Nottingham music champion Mark Del of website *NUSIC*.

Courtesy of Mark Del

Above: Jake in 2012, performing his support slot for soul singer Michael Kiwanuka. This was Jake's first tour and the first time he'd ever been outside of the UK.

Below: Jake on the Pyramid Stage at Glastonbury in 2013.

It's not often a photographer catches Jake with a smile – perhaps it's because the photo was taken on the set of *The Jay Leno Show* in the US.

Left: Jason 'Jay' Hart in 2006. The Nottingham musician would become Jake's co-manager and mentor.   © *Rex Features*

Right: Jake and co-manager Jason Hart in 2013.

© *Rex Features*

Above: With model Cara Delevingne at an event organised by fashion house Burberry in 2013 – when the pair left together that night it turned Jake from an indie rocker into a target for the tabloids.
© *Getty Images*

Below left: With Rolling Stone Ronnie Wood at the *Q* Awards in 2013. Jake won Best New Act and his entire speech consisted of one word: 'Cheers...'
© *Getty Images*

Below right: Jake at the Ivor Novello Awards in London, 2013.
© *Getty Images*

white video was made to accompany the release – it was just Jake, his guitar, a microphone and a chair. It probably cost a fair amount but it was remarkably similar to the videos he shot for nothing for Zoe Kirk's *This Is Live…* only in black-and-white.

When 'Lightning Bolt' was released as the follow-up, it was indeed a game changer – it became a Top 30 hit in the UK. It was accompanied by another shaky, super-8 style video by Michael Holyk, shot on various European locations including Belgium and The Netherlands, where the song also charted. 'It was very instinctive,' Bugg said when asked about writing the song. 'We just played what felt right. I think songs should write themselves – and that song wrote itself. Sometimes you have to sit down and work with a song but that song was a natural thing.'

Jake was now overground, on TV and on Radio 1, and Nottingham was fizzing with the news of Jake's success. Zoe Kirk: 'The thing with the Nottingham music scene, people are always tweeting, "Listen out who's going to be on Radio 1 this afternoon," and so on. Hearing Fearne Cotton introduce him was just bonkers, just amazing. To be talking about him with such high regard saying she loved his music, this new guy from Nottingham, you should check him out – that was great. To think I'd been chatting to him when he was doing his local gigs, the next breath he's on mainstream radio. Incredible.'

Reviewers were taken aback by the crackerjack, three-chord energy of the precocious singer's single. 'I'm pretty sure it's slightly unfair on established folk singers that Jake Bugg has managed such an authentic sound at the ripe age of 18,' said *Theregoesthefear* website. Referencing Bugg's hero Johnny Cash and one of his classic 1950s singles, the review continued 'Hailing from Nottingham, he was born in possibly the place furthest away from Folsom State Prison. As short in length as the name would suggest, "Lightning Bolt" is the follow-up single to Radio 1 favourite "Trouble Town". The track is driven by a riff not too dissimilar from his debut, but goes great with the troubadour's sixtiesesque vocals. "Lightning Bolt" is a step on from "Trouble Town", which was a Dylan-influenced comment on the Nottingham estates he grew up on. A summer hit, Jake's new single is immensely enjoyable.'

It appeared that Jake could rock as well as strum – and so could Nottingham. Helped by the success of Jake and other musicians, the city was on the up. In May local businessman Tony Bates managed to get *#NottinghamRocks* trending worldwide. Local stars like Torvill and Dean and *Gavin and Stacy* actor Matt Horne got involved, as did actress Vicky McClure, who was gearing up for an appearance on one of Jake's videos. 'Just woke up from a night shoot (very spaced out) to load of tweets about #Nottinghamrocks!!!' she tweeted. 'It does!!!! My fav hashtag yet!! X'.

By now, Jake had embarked on his first ever tour, supporting British soul singer Michael Kiwanuka – it was a big move in more ways than one; the dates took him out of the UK for the first time. 'I got to go to Milan and Sweden…

all over really. I think the biggest crowd on the tour was 1,500 people in Amsterdam. In Stockholm there were only 650 people but they were all completely silent, listening to me. And that's pretty incredible for a support act. It was weird to experience all the different cultures, although they're not too different to us.'

For Jake's dad David, this was the point where his son's career began to really kick in: 'He went on tour with Michael Kiwanuka around Europe,' he told the *Nottingham Post*. 'It was probably then that I realised that he was going to be mega.'

On the UK dates, reviewers from outside Nottingham started to get their first taste of Jake Bugg. One review, from the *Liverpool Echo* for Sound City Festival, seemed to sum up the reaction Bugg was getting: 'Nottingham's Jake Bugg takes to the stage next and we're all blown away. This is what Sound City is all about. Acoustic guitar, drums and bass it may well be again... but Bugg has the intangible. The songs are ace, the playing immaculate and we're in the presence of something. New single "Lightning Bolt" comes on like Alex Turner's *Submarine* soundtrack and that Scott Walkeresque croon echoes around the old building. The star of Sound City 2012 may have just strutted off stage like Dylan finishing *"It's Alright, Ma"*. Yep, that good.' From the city that gave the world The Beatles, the *Echo* review must have gone down particularly well on the tour bus the following day. Memories of the tour would stay with Jake for a long time, as would his gratitude towards Michael

Kiwanuka – Bugg would make a point of performing Kiwanuka's song 'Tell Me a Tale' when success came the teenager's way.

Back home, Jake had festival slots coming up – Y Not in Derbyshire, and Dot to Dot (where Jake played a short, teatime slot at Nottingham Rock City) all appeared on his itinerary but a key moment was his highly symbolic appearance at Splendour in Nottingham. In the space of 12 months he'd graduated from bottom of the bill on the new artists' stage to the main stage. 'That was a shock, to be honest, because I was on The Courtyard Stage last year,' he told the *Nottingham Post*. 'To go to the main stage in the space of a year is incredible. I wasn't expecting that at all.'

On a blazing hot summer's day, Jake played before his home crowd: 'Local lad Jake Bugg kicked things off in style as reward for those who had headed to Wollaton Park for lunchtime,' is how his local paper the *Nottingham Post* covered the show. 'Promoted to the main stage this year, Bugg showed exactly why he's a star on the rise. With his latest EP "Taste It" sitting pretty in the iTunes Top Five and a US tour with Noel Gallagher on the horizon, Clifton boy Jake set the bar high with his tight 30-minute set before giving the people what they wanted and cracking hit "Lightning Bolt".

For Splendour promoter George Akins, Bugg's move up the bill was a recognition of the hard work the teenager had put in: 'He went from the small show that we did at Splendour on The Courtyard, onto the main stage the year after – "Lightning Bolt" had been on a TV advert, he'd been getting B-listed and C-listed on radio, but I think the advert really started getting people noticing. Jake played a lot – he played the Acoustic Rooms, he played the Glee Club a lot, he did a residency at the Glee Club for a period. We did an acoustic night at the Rescue Rooms, he played there a few times. He played at Bodega – he did the progression. It happened quicker than most, he had a good year of playing the small acoustic shows and everything, but it happened quickly.'

It was a great achievement – but NUSIC's Mark Del, acting as master of ceremonies at Splendour, had another thing on his mind. He was still campaigning for the elusive Nottingham Number One. He decided to seize the moment: 'I stood on that stage at Splendour and said, "I think Jake Bugg will get a Number One album," in front of 15,000 people.'

At the time, this must have seemed like a slightly bizarre statement – hyperbole even by Del's standards. Jake Bugg was good... but was he *that* good?

CHAPTER TEN

KITCHEN-SINK DRAMA

Soundtrack:
The Stone Roses – 'Fools Gold' 1989
Longpigs – 'On and On' 1996
Noel Gallagher's High Flying Birds – 'The Death of You and Me' 2011

With Mark Del's words ringing across a slightly baffled Splendour crowd – a Number One album? Bugg? Really? – Jake left the stage. But he left it in a strong position. His new EP was called *Taste It*; the release seemed intended to reflect its title – it would act as a sampler for the album that was to come.

The title track was reminiscent again of an Arctic Monkeys twangathon via Liverpool band The La's, one of the acts that Jason Hart had worked with in the past. The song acted as a guide post between Jake's last release and the song that would follow it, 'Two Fingers'. 'We had "Lightning Bolt" and we had "Two Fingers",' he told *Face Culture*. 'We needed a song that kind of linked those two songs together because they were going to be the singles. So I wrote "Taste It" with Ian. I wasn't too sure about it but once it was finished I thought: That's all right, that. It's kinda just what we needed. It's kind of about being on the road and being away from everything and saying bye to your loved ones. It's about how you can get a taste for the road. I love the road, it's great.'

'Taste It' was backed by three other songs to make it like a good old-fashioned four-track EP. Next track 'Kentucky' is a slightly slower strut – it's a song written by Jake back at his mum's house in Clifton, where he would try to look beyond the four walls and the street outside to imagine a world and a life outside of his experience. '"Kentucky" is a song I wrote in my room,' he later told Radio 1. 'It was set in a place that was very different to where I was.' This method of imagining the big wide world did have its drawbacks though: 'I remember once, I thought: I'll look out the window for a bit of inspiration and the guy in the house across the road walked out of his shower stark naked!'

'Love Me The Way You Do' is that old Bugg favourite, this time with a slightly distracting accompaniment of oompah bass and slide guitar – it was probably better left as it was. 'Green Man' puts things back on track with shimmery guitars, Ringo Starr-style drums and far out lyrics.

'Notts newcomer Bugg is undoubtedly the best of the bunch in 2012 when it comes to channelling the great lineage of British pop into his own concoctions,' said the *NME* in the early throws of a love affair with Bugg and his music. '"Taste It" is his finest tune yet, beginning with a fine burst of La's guitar, bass that's pure Entwistle [John Entwistle of The Who], Lennonesque snarl and finally – triumphantly – a Noely G one-note solo. Ya get the picture?'

'Bugg is astoundingly self-assured, his musical ability is versatile and of the very highest calibre, but the most fascinating thing about him is that he sings with an unexpected sophistication for one so young,' said the review of the EP on the *Unambitious Us* website. 'This EP is just the start – Jake Bugg's debut album is, dare I say, the most eagerly anticipated of the year and, providing he doesn't change a thing, will compete amongst the greats he has so deservedly earned comparisons to.'

Idol magazine reported, 'Following the no-fuss and no-frills style of his previous singles, "Trouble Town" and "Lightning Bolt", the latter of which is making Jake Bugg a regular radio-airtime fixture, the teenage blues-rock purist continues his one-man mission for some straightforward rock'n'roll stimulation with his latest single "Taste It". The title track from his debut EP, which is set to be released in August, is a short and sharp demonstration of Bugg's raw vocal talents, and his admirable commitment to channelling his timeless influences of Johnny Cash and the early years of The Beatles.'

To maintain the momentum, Bugg had a slew of festival gigs planned for the summer of 2012 – Y Not Festival in Derbyshire, Reading and Leeds, Bestival and Into The Great Wide Open in Holland. But it was some carefully cultivated support slots that would put him very much in the right kind of company – and in front of the right kind of audiences – to broaden his appeal. Ian Brown of The Stone Roses seemed to share the same physical and musical DNA as Bugg – it was a fair bet that if you liked Brown, you'd be into Bugg. It was a smart move to get Jake to support the newly revitalised Stone Roses that summer, including an opening slot at a star-studded 'secret' gig at the Village Underground venue in East London. The pre-Olympics show was sponsored by Adidas – a very Buggesque type of clothing – and a host of sports stars attended: 'Arriving at the Adidas Underground, the streets are already thronged with blaggers, chancers and sundry other individuals ready to twist somebody's arm in order to gain entry,' said the review of the show in *Clash* magazine. 'Pushing through the door, you're met with a dank heat, the packed crowd bobbing under the arches. Bradley Wiggins is here. He's posing for the press, tucked up in his tonic suit and slim knit tie. Paul Weller is here. Olympian Jessica Ennis is here. The Clash's own Mick Jones is here… hell, even Goldie is here amongst the packed faces and crowded limbs.'

Bugg himself seemed less phased by the celebs than he was by being in the same room as The Stone Roses. 'It was incredible,' he told Fearne Cotton on Radio 1. 'I never ever thought I'd get to see The Stones Roses live, so to play on the same stage as them... it was a great night. They're really nice lads. Ian was like, "You're very brave singing those kind of songs." Which was a bit mad.' Jake also got to meet Led Zeppelin's Jimmy Page but, instead of asking the guitarist about his time with one of the biggest rock bands of all time, Bugg quizzed him about his work with his hero Donovan – Page played on tracks like 'Sunshine Superman'.

A few weeks later he supported ex-Oasis star Noel Gallagher at a low-key gig at Dingwalls in London for the charity War Child. 'It was nice to be asked,' Gallagher said. 'I'm doing my bit for the kids and little Jake Bugg is opening for me. He's great. I'm kind of a YouTube fan of his.' The War Child gig was the first time the two had met – like Ian Brown, Gallagher is a living advertisement for moochy swagger and, for a Nottingham lad, Bugg seemed to have a surprising amount of that Mancunian vibe in his system. This small show later blossomed into a full-on invite for Jake to open for Gallagher's band High Flying Birds in Europe and the US. 'Noel's obviously an idol of mine, so meeting him – you do have to pinch yourself a bit, but you just come to realise they're normal people at the end of the day,' Jake told the BBC. 'Like, he came backstage to meet us and said, "Y'alright, nice to meet you all, where did you get them trainers from?"'

After the show, the *NME* arranged for the pair to have their photo taken together – there was a sense of a torch being passed on from Gallagher to Bugg. 'We were sat on the step together having our photo taken,' Bugg said, 'and Noel says to me, "Come closer, I'm not going to bite." But you know when you've come offstage and you're all sweaty? You don't want to put your fucking arm around someone straightaway! He's not given me any advice yet but we've got a whole tour to do so who knows? It was a big gig tonight though. When I was 14, I got well into Oasis. As a song-writer, Noel's a total legend.'

For an Americana enthusiast like Jake, going to the States with Gallagher was a massive deal – though he travelled second class while Noel was up front in first: 'Going to America is a dream come true,' he told his local paper the *Nottingham Post*. 'I think the places I'm looking forward to the most are Nashville and Texas. A lot of the music I like comes from those American states.'

Iain Archer's former colleagues Snow Patrol were also booked on the tour as co-headliners with Gallagher's band High Flying Birds – not everyone was impressed by this pairing: 'Snore patrol Noel Gallaghers high flying smurfs who said rock'n'roll is dead,' tweeted Noel's brother Liam.

One of the stipulations for touring with Gallagher was that Bugg was going to have to leave his backing band behind and go back to the old days – it would be just him and his guitar: 'Unfortunately, I can't take the band, which is a bit crap, but it's still going to be an amazing tour, I'm sure,' he told *Music Radar* website. 'It's just going to be me and the guitar. I was doing that for a few years before I met the band so it's just like being back to my roots really.'

Meanwhile, the final touches were being put on Jake's

album. 'I'm quite close to finishing writing it,' he said. 'It's taken me about six months, which I'm really pleased about because it takes some about a year or two years to finish an album. Although some of the songs I already had. They were the ones that helped me get the deal. People have been comparing me to Bob Dylan and he is amazing, don't get me wrong, but maybe a lot of people say that because they don't really know Donovan.'

Meanwhile, more songwriting 'mentors' had been brought on board to contribute to his debut. Crispin Hunt was drafted in as the co-writer and producer of one track, 'Broken'. At one stage, Hunt seemed to have the 1990s all sewn up. As lead singer of Britpop also-rans Longpigs – the band's guitarist was future hitmaker Richard Hawley – Hunt racked up a small handful of hits and a great deal of press attention before the band split in the year 2000. Since then, Hunt had worked with the likes of Mark Owen, Florence + The Machine and Ellie Goulding as both a writer and producer. It's likely that Hunt was the first person called Crispin that Jake had ever come across – that name being in short supply in Clifton. Jake recalled spending time with the Longpigs' singer to finish off the song: 'He had this big Georgian house with, like, fucking chandeliers!' he told Q magazine, proving that, although you can take the boy out of Clifton, the reverse is a more difficult manoeuvre. 'And there's me just come from me estate and eating, like, *baked salmon* with these doctors he had round for dinner going, "Hmmm, ya, Crispin." I'm sitting there thinking: This is mad!'

Also on board for Bugg's debut was Matt Prime, whose CV was of a far more mainstream nature; he'd collaborated with Liberty X, Will Young, Olly Murs and Victoria Beckham in the past and came on board for Bugg's album to work on a track called 'Simple As This'. The fact that Prime had the kind of background in music that Bugg considered to be '*X Factor* shit' would make this hook-up an easy target for Jake's critics when the album was released. In fact, the presence of Hunt, Prime and the overall guiding hand of Iain Archer caused a great deal of suspicion in some quarters. 'I'm still very young and I should soak up what I can learn from people with more experience,' Bugg told the *Daily Star* by way of explanation. 'I'm taking it on board, so I can step into writing on my own eventually.'

In the end, four songs on Jake's debut would come with only his name attached to them – all the other tracks would be co-writes. This is something that those keen to test Bugg's authenticity would return to again and again. It appears that Jake himself needed convincing too: 'I have to be honest, I got sceptical at first,' he later admitted to journalist Tony Clayton-Lea. 'As an artist you can be defensive – you know, what's wrong with my songs? But I had to take a step back, analyse the situation and realise that at the age of 17 I might just be able to learn from someone like Iain [Archer]. He's been doing it for a long time, and he's good, and so it's a great experience for me to learn as much as I can so that in the future I won't need to write with anyone. That said, Iain is more of a mate now, not just someone I write songs with. For every two ideas I have he'll tell me which one he thinks is the best. It's good to have such an instinctive person around.'

As the album neared completion, Bugg was starting to pop up everywhere: the BBC gave 'Lightning Bolt' a boost when they used the track as an inevitable backing track to the build up to the 100m men's final starring Usain Bolt. 'I forgot all about the Olympics, to be honest,' Bugg told the *NME*. 'I heard rumours that it might be used and, when it was, it was just great. And when he won, that was a bonus to top it all off.'

By now Jake was even starting to do some fashion shoots – a less Bugg-like activity it was hard to imagine. 'I didn't let them dress me up or anything,' he reassured *The Independent*. 'No, no. I just wore what I bought yesterday: Burberry, a bit of Adidas, Lacoste, Ralph Lauren. If it looks good, I like it. I was always into fashion but I never had the money to buy stuff before. I'm trying to get all the best bits I can now, while I'm still able to, you know?'

He also had his photo taken by veteran rock photographer Kevin Westenberg, who'd snapped everyone from Bjork to Bon Jovi. Westenberg's pictures of Bugg – jacket zipped up, guitar case in hand, fag on the go – would appear on Jake's debut album. The terraced houses seen in the pictures look like the mean streets of Nottingham but are, in fact, in a posh road in London.

As a final taster for the album, the Beatlesesque 'Two Fingers' was released as a single in September. The video to accompany the track was a two-fingered backwards wave to his home town of Clifton. The Nottingham-shot video featured Jake strolling through the city with his guitar on his back, just like he did when his was touting for gigs when he first started out. Bugg and his mates spend their days in a haze of smoke before Jake gives the literal two fingers to Clifton and his warring parents and heads off to America. Just what he'd done in real life with Noel Gallagher and Snow Patrol. The song was one of several that seemed to walk something of a tightrope in terms of Jake's attitude to his home town – being proud of where you're from yet aching to reach beyond it: 'When you're growing up, you want to get away,' Jake told Nottingham journalist Simon Wilson. 'I think that's a feeling that everyone's experienced as a teenager. You want to go out, travel the world, see things for yourself. And luckily, I'm doing that through my music.'

The kitchen-sink drama video was directed by Jamie Thraves, who'd previously worked with bands like Radiohead, Blur and Glasvegas. Jake's violent, drunken dad is played by Craig Parkinson from TV shows like *Whitechapel* and *Misfits*, but best known to music fans for playing Manchester music mogul Tony Wilson in the Joy Division biopic *Control*. Bugg's mum is played by Nottingham actress Vicky McClure, most notable for her work with director Shane Meadows, particularly his *This Is England* trilogy. 'She's lovely,' Jake told the *Nottingham Post*. 'I had to do a bit of acting in it. We had to improvise. She's such a great actor and she really helped me with that.'

McClure actually bears a striking resemblance to Bugg's

real-life mum Leeysa, who didn't care for the finished video. 'Mum is very supportive in what I do, but that video is pretty close to the truth,' Jake told the *Pure Volume* website. 'So obviously, my mum was a little bit upset about it.'

As well as hanging about on street corners pulling on a variety of joints, Jake was required to do a bit of acting for the first time. Parkinson and McClure's scenes as Jake's highly volatile parents were shot in a terraced house in the Sneinton area of Nottingham, as Jake tries to come between his warring parents. 'Directors always want to exaggerate things a bit, but it's not so far off and a lot of people have that same life,' he said. 'It felt quite natural to act it out. I never had a bad upbringing though.'

The local media were constantly drawn to songs like 'Two Fingers' – were the two fingers of the title directed at Clifton and Nottingham? 'It's quite ironic really,' Jake told *East Midlands Today*. 'When I wrote the song, I was still living in Nottingham – I hadn't gotten out at all. By writing that song, it helped me progress and pursue my career.' Put another way, a song about escaping from Clifton helped Jake Bugg escape from Clifton.

The usual suspects got behind the single – Zane Lowe made it his Hottest Record in the World – but it only got to Number 28 in the charts. Perhaps it was time for Jake to get his album out and be judged on his songs as a whole?

As the release date of the album approached, Mark Del's *NUSIC* website urged Nottingham to get behind Bugg and his fellow local artists – this was not the time for gentle words. Del described the coming weeks as 'the most exciting month for Nottingham's music scene this Millennium, possibly ever'. He wrote, 'We haven't had an artist register a Top 40 album since *Pitchshifter* went to 35 in June 2000. This month three artists could do it, and hey, we might even get that hallowed Number One. October is packed full of potential incredible moments. We're expecting Dog Is Dead, Jake Bugg and Natalie Duncan to rack up a score of exciting media firsts in print, on the telly and on radio. Indeed in just 48 hours' time Jake will have his first session with Zane Lowe, definitely the first Nottingham solo artist to notch up this honour. Today BBC 6 Music has basically been Jake FM. So October is here. The month the most vibrant music scene in the UK steps it up. Be proud, and let's all do our bit.'

CHAPTER ELEVEN

WE ARE NOTTINGHAM

Soundtrack:
The Rolling Stones – 'Have You Seen Your Mother, Baby,
Standing in the Shadow?' 1966
John Denver – 'Sunshine On My Shoulders' 1973
Leona Lewis – 'Run' 2008

Jake's Bugg's debut album, released on 15 October 2012, is to be applauded, if nothing else, for the brevity of its 'thank you' section. In an age of endless name-checks for everyone from God to the person who said something quite nice to you in 2007, Bugg's take is refreshing and typically brief: 'To everyone who helped me get here, thanks a lot.'

It looks the part too – with its black-and-white cover, moody pics and retro Mercury Records imprint, *Jake Bugg* looks like it ought to sound: an album that's out of its time.

Sonically, the rockers are up front: 'Lightning Bolt', 'Two Fingers' and 'Taste It' appear one after the other. It's familiar, up-tempo fare that won't scare away the casual observer attracted by the singles. The mid-tempo 'Seen It All' is next, a new track that fits in perfectly with the character that the album has established during the previous three tracks – Bugg is cast as the slightly alienated observer, tugging on a joint as he watches life go by on the streets of Clifton. In 'Seen It All' – later a single – Bugg describes the pills, thrills and bellyaches of a Friday night out in Nottingham. It features knives, gangsters and a stabbing outside a party. It's a Bugg/Archer song, with Archer playing bass and guitar as well as producing. '"Seen It All", that's a true experience that I had,' he later said. 'It's quite graphic. I talk about taking things that maybe I shouldn't. It's not like I'm trying to promote it. I'm saying, I took this, it didn't go too well, don't do it.'

'Simple As This' is the song Jake wrote with mainstream writer and producer Matt Prime. Despite Prime's pop pedigree, this is the most Bugg-like song so far, a return to the simple country chords of Jake's Nottingham sessions after the rat-a-tat of the opening salvo. It's Jake in reflective mode, trying to make his way in life but realising he's over-complicating things – the song and the tone of Bugg's voice bring to mind John Denver's 'Sunshine On My Shoulders', an album track that was released as a single for the chirpy country star in 1973. The simplicity of the track is a good primer for 'Country Song', one of four songs credited solely to Jake, a Bugg bedroom song from back in Clifton. The temptation must have been considerable to put some whistles and bells on the track but that's resisted here. It remains what it always was: a three-chord country song about imagining yourself somewhere greener and more pleasant than a council house in Clifton.

Next is 'Broken' – written with chandelier-loving musician Crispin Hunt – again keeping things slow and easy. The version here is the original demo with added instrumentation and a fake choir. Guitars and some rimshot drums are all we get to start with but this song is a 'builder' – it takes its time and it's the longest track here and builds to what songwriters refer to as the 'lift': the moment when a tune kicks in and takes off. 'You can hear it building up and you know it's coming,' said Bugg. 'I don't always like to do the expected but sometimes you have to give people what they think they're going to hear. Satisfaction, you might say.'

Things are taken up a notch with 'Trouble Town', Bugg's first single and another one of his 'get me out of Clifton' songs. In the context of the album, the short sharp song acts as a swift break from the slower songs. If *Jake Bugg* was an old fashioned vinyl album – which is what it strives to be – this would signify the start of side two. 'Ballad of Mr Jones' is a 'murder ballad', a style of song favoured by Bugg's hero Johnny Cash. A typical example would see the details of a terrible crime being played out, with the wrongdoer often – but not always – receiving their comeuppance by the final verse. In 'Ballad of Mr Jones', a blind man is put in the frame for a murder he didn't commit, as the real perpetrators go free. It's still typically short and sweet and might have benefitted from stretching out into a longer form, but it's a fascinating glimpse at the kind of songs that Bugg and Archer might be capable of.

'Slide' is Bugg doing his best Liam Gallagher with a soaring vocal that he had to get in one take because of the difficulty in hitting the bigger notes. 'That song is difficult for me to sing,' he said. 'It's very hard on the voice, so I went into the studio knowing I'm going to have to nail it first take, because after that [the voice] just gets weaker and weaker.'

'Someone Told Me' is old-school Bugg, a song he performed on *This Is Live* with Zoe Kirk. The tale of a girl who had the temerity to fall for someone else, it remains true to its roots – it was a simple song, with Jake plus guitar and that's how it's presented here.

'Note To Self' exhibits more by way of musical garnish, with the addition of strings, in particular, making the track stand out. Here, Bugg sings a little lower than elsewhere on the album. It's a straightforward 'don't be so hard on yourself' affair and it could come from a 1970s album from Glenn Campbell or, again, John Denver.

'Someplace' is a solo Bugg composition and the oldest song on the album. Written when Jake was just 15, he felt that the naïve lyrics and basic chord structure might make it sit uncomfortably with other songs on the album, but he was overruled by the record company. They were right and he was wrong and it's an important link to Bugg's past and the kind of song he played when he was gigging at The Maze.

The final track is 'Fire', recorded by Jake on his iPhone – it would be a perfectly pleasant, skanking end to the album if it weren't for the addition of a rubbish crackling vinyl effect to give a deliberately aged feel. That aside, Bugg was delighted that a self-recorded piece made the cut: 'I get the producer credit – buzzin!' Actually, the track is listed in the sleeve notes as having been 'recorded' by Jake Bugg rather than having been 'produced' by him. Sorry, Jake.

It would be an understatement to say that the album took reviewers by surprise: 'Jake Bugg's debut album is almost too good to be true,' gasped the *Daily Mail*. Describing him as a 'teenager in love with the fifties', reviewer Tim De Lisle took the opportunity to point out that The Beatles, The Stones and Bob Dylan all looked backwards before they looked forwards – so don't get waylaid by concerns over Bugg's lack of originality: 'His look is that of a mid-sixties pop star – dark fringe, cute face, a hint of attitude and vulnerability. But his sound comes straight from the late fifties. Fresh, clear and uncluttered, it is mostly just a voice (nasal twang, crisp diction) and a guitar (a Telecaster, bustling, bursting with life). It's as if Buddy Holly had grown up on a council estate in the East Midlands. The 14 songs here are short, sharp and engaging. The fast ones are rock'n'roll with a touch of folk or blues, while the slow ones lean towards country. These are old, old forms, and many of today's teenagers have given up on them, preferring hip-hop, dance music or indie. But Bugg makes them young again, and adds a dollop of contemporary jadedness (one song is entitled "Seen It All") that takes him close to the best of Noel Gallagher.'

The *Daily Mail* loved it – so that was the oldies on board. What about the young 'uns? 'Authenticity is the last meaningful currency left in indie,' opined the *NME*. 'These days we tend not to focus on whether our pop stars are doing things we haven't heard before, but instead on what their education cost and how many failed musical adventures they had before getting famous (please see: The Vaccines, Mumford & Sons, Spector). Jake Bugg needn't worry about that. For one thing, at just 18 years old, he's barely had time to be a failed anything. For another, having grown up in Clifton, formerly the largest housing estate in Europe, he's more likely to nick silver spoons than choke on them. Mostly though, it's because he's a frighteningly talented songwriter. Whisper it, in case the weight of expectation proves too heavy, but he's the real deal.'

The praise for Bugg's debut album was widespread – but not complete. *The Guardian*'s view was, 'Jake Bugg sounds like he could be a box-ticking exercise for a cynical major label: Hey! We need us one of those acoustic types that are doing so well – but let's get one who'll appeal to the kids who like The View more than Ed Sheeran! So here's a young man singing about necking pills in car parks and stabbings at parties to a backing that alternates between beaty pop reminiscent of The La's and acoustic fingerpicking, the link being his nasal voice, uncannily reminiscent of La's leader

Lee Mavers. He's not quite there yet – his slice-of-life lyrics tend to the over-literal, and once he's hit on a stirring riff, as on the single, "Lightning Bolt", he seems to feel the job is done. But there's an attractive openness to the album, with no sense of contrivance: he's singing about what he knows. Once he knows a little more, you get the sense he might manage something truly memorable.'

Outside of the reviewers, there were other opinions to be had: those of the people back in Nottingham who had, in the words of the album's brief 'thank you' section, helped get him here. 'I loved the album straight away,' Dean Jackson of BBC Radio Nottingham told me. 'I don't think there's a bad track on the album myself. I think there's some quite emotional stuff on there, there's some rocky stuff on there. I enjoyed the album tremendously, that's not me saying it as someone who was instrumental in the early days of Jake. I genuinely liked it.'

'I think the sequencing of the album is very strange,' Mike Atkinson, who wrote that key first national feature on Jake, told me. 'I think it's better when you play it backwards actually. It's interesting; he actually starts his set with "Fire" these days. I think it was a mistake to front load it with bangers, I thought that was a record company move. It's sequenced for iTunes, rather than a complete listening experience. I think the album works better as a cohesive record once you get the bangers out of the way. I often start playing it from about track four or five, it works better from there. I might go back to the bangers at the end, like he'd play it at the end of his set. I like playing them at the end of the album from a listening point of view.'

Gaz Peacham from The Maze, where Jake started his playing career: 'I think he refined his sound when his album came out. When I heard his album for the first time, I was like, "Wow, that's not quite how I remembered it!" He obviously had been guided slightly, given advice and it had been polished up, but he's done it well.'

That sense of Bugg being 'polished up' by the record company would linger – it especially irked people who objected to the presence of Iain Archer and the other songwriters. Dean Jackson: 'Jake's been very open about who he's worked with on the album, he's never tried to bury that and he's spoken very eloquently about people he's worked with – he's called them his friends. That will be the way it's been presented to him: here's someone who's going to help you with your craft. So I don't have a problem with it at all. A lot of the songs that are co-writes, I heard them in their early days before Jake met these people. If anyone has the idea that somebody else wrote the songs for him, they're very mistaken.'

For Jackson, if the likes of Iain Archer being involved meant the album got done and came out the way it did... so be it: 'If a 17-year-old is trying to write a whole album on his own in the first instance, what's it going to end up like?' Jackson says. 'Would it have gone in at Number One? No. Would it be nominated for Mercury? Unlikely. So I don't have a problem with that and there have been a few conversations in the pub over this, I must admit. And there are some people who seem very hung up on that, but I look at it like this. Suppose Jake had nothing to do with the writing process at all? Suppose all the songs had been written for him and presented to him? I would still think it's a good album – it's a well-sung album and well-performed album. Maybe I'm biased but, to me, the songs on the album are great. It was an album that was released quite quickly and I think it could have had a lot more polish put on it, but I think it would have been the wrong thing to do. We needed the sort of rawness that we hear with Jake.'

Fellow musicians rallied around Bugg – they were willing him to succeed: 'Just grabbed @JakeBugg's new album. Great tunes,' tweeted Ed Sheeran, someone you would expect to have a very similar record collection to Jake's. 'All about the @JakeBugg album,' said dance act Chase and Status. 'New @JakeBugg album is superb,' added Example. 'Check it out people. Talented little fucker he is.'

Shortly after the album's release, there was fairly confident talk of it going straight into the Top Ten. Then the people of Nottingham started to think the unthinkable: could it go in the charts at Number One? 'Can the kid from Clifton, Jake Bugg, beat Leona Lewis to claim Number One?' implored the headline in the *Nottingham Post*. 'The latest figures show that there are only a few thousand copies between Jake Bugg's self-titled debut album and *Glassheart* by Leona Lewis. But Jake is in the lead, after hitting the Number One spot in the midweek album charts. And if the 18-year-old beats the superstar to claim the top of the album chart tomorrow, it will be a first for the city.'

'It feels great,' says Jake. 'Whether it will still be Number One when the chart comes out I don't know but it would be amazing. Especially with my debut album. I didn't imagine that it would get in the Top Ten, never mind Number One.'

Leona Lewis had released *Glassheart* three days earlier and, when it became clear that it was going to be neck and neck between the girl from *X Factor* and the boy who'd vowed to rid the charts of the very music she represented, Nottingham new music drumbeater Mark Del's site swung into action. His *NUSIC* website produced electronic flyers to be posted on social media, declaring MUSIC NEEDS YOU... and STOP LEONA!

'I know that she's off *X Factor*,' Jake told the *Nottingham Post* when asked about what he knew of his rival, 'and she probably doesn't write any of her songs.'

Not everyone approved, particularly when it was pointed out that one of Lewis's biggest hits was 'Run', the Snow Patrol song co-written by Iain Archer. Journalist Mike Atkinson: 'He was quite outspoken about Leona Lewis in interviews at the time,' Atkinson told me. 'I thought it was a mistake actually – I rolled my eyes. She's just "manufactured pop", yes, but you write with a guy from Snow Patrol. You co-write, ironically, with the guy who's written one of Leona Lewis's biggest hits! I don't like it when people try to play that authenticity card, it always annoys me. I think it's an overvalued concept.'

When the news was announced that Jake Bugg had entered

the chart at the top slot, beating Leona Lewis, Bugg's response was typically low-key: 'The whole city has got behind it, been really supportive and I'm very grateful for that. It feels cool, you know. I'm just a bit tired. I'm chilling out. It's mad, isn't it?'

The battle lines had been drawn and music writers seeking what they saw as authenticity found their champion in the shape of Jake Bugg: 'Are Bugg and his guitar-toting peers actually keeping "that *X Factor* shit" off Number One?' asked *NME* blogger Matthew Horton. 'Apart from the immediate effect – consigning Lewis's new album *Glassheart* to a lowly Number Three – there are signs Bugg and his indie/rock brethren have got a tightening stranglehold on the charts. Why? How? What can it all mean? Let's struggle to answer all that. Bugg is the sixth rock/indie/alt act in a row to take the UK Number One album spot, following The Vaccines, The xx, The Killers, Mumford & Sons and Muse (and the Mumfords again). Two's company, three's a crowd, six is a seismic shift in the cultural landscape. It says here. Anyway, it's an eye-catching development in a year that's seen the albums peak dominated by Adele, Emeli Sandé, Ed Sheeran, Adele again and a bit more Emeli Sandé.'

'I guess it proves my point,' Bugg concurred. 'People still want to hear guitar music. It's my job to keep that *X Factor* shit off the top of the charts.' Soon after he was told the news, he phoned his mum Leeysa: 'To think that he has achieved Number One in the albums chart fills me with such pride,' she said. 'I could hardly sleep I was so excited. And I think he has made not just myself and my family proud, but the whole of Nottingham.'

What had seemed like a far-flung idea – getting Nottingham's act back to the top of the charts – had been achieved. *NUSIC* rabble-rouser Mark Del, the man behind the campaign, had been right. Even he seemed shocked: 'We did this whole thing of "Dreaming of a Nottingham Number One", thing since 2008, that's been the tagline. It could have been horrendous. Can you imagine some Crazy Frog tribute band could have gotten to Number One? As it is, we've produced one of the most incredible breakthrough artists in the last 12 months. It's a wet dream! But it could have gone horribly wrong.'

Rather brilliantly, once they got the Number One that the city so clearly wanted, the *Nottingham Post* ran an article about the many and varied chart successes the area had actually achieved over the years: Corinne Drewery of Swing Out Sister was born in Beeston, Jay McGuiness from The Wanted is from Newark, Stereo MCs grew up in Ruddington and Bruce Dickinson of Iron Maiden is from Worksop. So there.

For many it seemed like Bugg was the people's pop star, slaying the corporate music beast with just a guitar, a few tunes and a moochy shrug. Music journalist Mike Atkinson: 'I talk a lot about music to friends who have only a passing interest in music – and they have even less interest in Nottingham music – but I became aware that a kind of organic support was building for Jake. By the time his album came out, everyone that I knew knew of him and everyone I knew loved it really loved him, they really warmed to him. It's one of those rare instances where an act gets to Number One through quite a nice, organic, everyone actually being really into the music sort of thing, rather than the hyped thing. I'm sure everyone thought that Leona Lewis was going to go to Number One. It was the sort of the phenomenon you got with Elbow's *Seldom Seen Kid* about five years ago – it's word of mouth, people just genuinely connecting.'

As 2012 came to an end – remember, Bugg was gigging in the car park of The Peacock this time the previous year – he was asked by the *Nottingham Post* to reflect on what had happened to him: 'It's been a bit of a mad year, to be honest,' Jake told the paper that had followed his career from the very start. 'But if you think about such a dramatic rise to success too much, it would probably distract you. You have to keep thinking about the next thing, the next song you're going to write, how you're going to move forward. It has been a brilliant year though. But you've got to live it, rather than analyse it. When I was growing up, this is what I wanted to do and, when you're sitting in your bedroom as a teenager working out songs and practising constantly, you dream of success all the time. This sounds odd but, when success actually happens, you've had it in your head for so many years it doesn't actually feel that weird. It did feel like I'd been working towards it since I was about 12. That so many people have liked the album so quickly is the strange thing. I can only put that down to those who started following me liked what they heard and told other people. Perhaps my timing was right but it wasn't planned or anything. We certainly won't know whether anything comes of this increased interest for another year or so. We'll just have to see how it goes.'

A few weeks later, Jake returned to Nottingham, playing at the city's Rescue Rooms venue. Journalist Mike Atkinson was there to review the show, saying, 'We knew this one was going to be special. A month after topping the album charts with his debut album, in its first week of release, 18-year-old Clifton lad Jake Bugg returned to Nottingham in triumph, for his big homecoming show. Jake's success has a special significance for Nottingham. Almost unbelievably, he is the first home-grown act ever to score a Number One album; an achievement which is long overdue, to put it mildly. Nurtured by a supportive, confident and ever-expanding music community within the city, his success has shown other local acts that anything is possible. Unfazed as ever by his sudden good fortune, Jake took the homecoming hero's welcome in his stride. "It's great to be back," he murmured, his expression betraying nothing more than a steady focus on getting the job done. Stage patter just isn't his style, you see.'

After a swift 50-minute set, Jake left the stage. The crowd wanted him to return for an encore. It's traditional to shout 'More' on such occasions... to whistle, to clap and to cheer. The crowd at the Rescue Rooms didn't do that. They chanted, 'We are Nottingham... We are Nottingham... We are Nottingham!'

CHAPTER TWELVE

WHEN POSH TOTTY MEETS POP GROTTY

Soundtrack:
Hank Williams – 'Honky Tonkin'' 1948
Squeeze – 'Goodbye Girl' 1978
The Strypes – 'Blue Collar Jane' 2013

After getting to Number One, Jake went on a hefty night out with his record label before heading off to America with Noel Gallagher and Iain Archer's old mates Snow Patrol. The tour started in Portland, Oregon and ended in Houston two and a half weeks later. Jake was back down to the bottom of the bill and many reviewers didn't arrive early enough to catch him. Those that did didn't seem to quite know what to make of him: 'His guitar-accompanied songs were very nice, but his nasal voice made them all sound too similar,' said the *Seattle Music Insider*.

'America was brilliant,' Jake later told the BBC. 'It felt like you're in a film set when you're there. One of the best shows I played was at The Ryman in Nashville. The likes of Hank Williams, Johnny Cash and Dolly Parton have played there. You can feel the atmosphere. That was quite overwhelming, to be honest. That was a brilliant show. I saw some great guitars as well.'

The *NME* travelled out to see the tour and reported that, at some shows, audiences were 'worryingly sparse'. But given that Bugg was a completely unknown quantity in North America, the responsibility for ticket sales lay very much with Gallagher and Snow Patrol. It might have been enough to drive Gallagher to drink but, according to Bugg, the former Oasis guitarist and renowned party animal was now a changed man: 'Noel is looking after himself, making sure he has plenty of rest and stuff,' Jake told *The Sun*. 'We've had a couple of drinks, but not too many though as obviously we're on the road and have to try and be healthy... I try my best but being 18 it can be quite difficult. We have to make sure we get enough sleep, get practice in and don't ruin our voices.'

Jake had left quite a buzz behind him in the UK after he'd hit Number One and defeated the menace of '*X Factor* shit'. The talent show was on air in Britain and journalists could smell a story. And they got one. Jake became the go-to guy if you wanted someone to slag off generic pop music and the people who made it. 'Loads of people have given me shit about that stuff I said about *X Factor*,' he told the *NME*. 'Little fans saying snidey comments. They don't bother me. I find it quite funny actually. At the end of the day, it's about who they think the public will like most. And that's how they choose. If I'd have gone on it, I wouldn't have been Number One. OK, maybe if I had have gone on that show, hypothetically, I might get to Number One. But I wouldn't have any ownership of the songs. These people, you put a sheet of music in front of them and they'll sing it. They don't care. They're not singing the song, man. And that's disgraceful.'

But it was Bugg's comments about One Direction that really kicked things off. In response to a gentle prodding about the *X Factor*-spawned group being the closest thing we have to rock stars these days, he told journalist Jimi Famurewa in *Shortlist* magazine that they, 'must know they're terrible. They must know. Calling them the new rock stars is a ridiculous statement. And people should stop making it.'

This was exactly what the media wanted – Jake Bugg, the authentic, guitar-toting voice of council-estate Britain, versus the soft-pop puppets of manufactured music. 'I don't care about the word "pop",' he told *Q* magazine. 'The Beatles were pop, it's just what's popular. But sadly, what's popular today is mostly manufactured and commercial and all about fame and looks and boy bands. It's not on. One Direction? The young girls will grow up and forget about 'em. There's only one [direction] they'll be going after that, isn't there? Down. I'm interested in which songs, artists, will be remembered in fifty years' time.'

Journalists everywhere were rubbing their hands with glee when the One Direction lads responded: 'Hi @JakeBugg do you think slagging off boy bands makes you more indie?' asked Louis Tomlinson on Twitter. Band mate Niall Horan went one better – adding some devastating wordplay to his comeback: 'Really buggs me that artists we're fans of, flip on us in the press!' he tweeted. Clever.

Bugg, not unreasonably, questioned why One Direction were being mentioned in the same breath as 'proper' music: 'I don't know how they can really be considered a band though, to be honest,' he said. 'I'm not too sure. I think the more I play on it, it'll wind them up. They're there to look good. Music-wise? I assume they don't really have a clue. We'll just see. They might do. Probably the ugliest one is the best singer. He might know a couple of chords.'

Putting the boot into One Direction became something of a knee-jerk reaction for Bugg – it was as if he couldn't help himself. Even when trying to be diplomatic, he still managed to twist the knife. When asked if he was going to respond to the tweets, particularly as one of One Direction had declared himself a fan, Jake told *Newsbeat*, 'Not everyone is going to be a fan. They might have kind of liked my music but I try and write my own songs. As a songwriter it's very hard to listen to music that's not coming from the heart and soul personally. I'm not going to get involved in tweeting back because that's ridiculous.'

In a rerun of great pop clashes of the past – Beatles versus Stones, Blur versus Oasis – the Great British Public were invited to take sides. Heavyweight pundits like Paul Morley of *The Guardian*, in typically contrary fashion, weighed in on behalf of One Direction: 'If pop is all about the pose, the masquerade, then [Harry] Styles is way out in front; Bugg stuck in a square rock'n'roll past now as quaint-seeming as George Formby, Styles effortlessly streaming through the liquid entertainmentscape as modern as a ruined reputation, a Piers Morgan insult or a food scandal. It's difficult to appreciate if you might pine for the sixties of the Stones or the nineties of Oasis but, as things are now, Styles is the truth – authentic, perversely sophisticated, a groomed blank symbol of what's left of pop, the daily hype, monstrous turnover and aimless, targeted pressure. Bugg is the plastic, phoney contestant, a weedy echo of an echo of an echo of the idea that to write your own songs based on personal experience of a local world and a wider universe can lead to genius.'

If Morley seemed to prefer the style of Harry over that of Bugg, it was nothing compared to the way Jake seemed to annoy some critics: 'For those of us who occasionally strive to defend heritage-minded, guitar-based indie rock from critics who would gleefully dance on its graves, Jake Bugg is a real bummer,' Emeli Mackay wrote in *The Independent*. 'He plays into all the worst stereotypes, with his surly po-face, his sexless unaesthetic, his narrow opinions on *X Factor*, One Direction, Taylor Swift and the importance in Our Troubled Times of proper songs, played on real instruments, crafted from the wood of integrity trees felled in the Forest Of Authenticity. Never mind that his debut album was co-written with former members of Snow Patrol and Longpigs and he got his big break on a beer advert.'

But Bugg proved he could give it as well as he could take it. For someone who doesn't say a great deal, Jake became quite adept at tossing out casual put-downs of other acts – such as the following examples. Teenage blues band The Strypes (who are on the same record label as he is): 'When they write some fucking tunes, we'll talk, eh?' Mumford & Sons: 'They just look like posh farmers with banjos to me.' Even the Brit Awards got a pasting, after Jake was nominated for Best Breakthrough Act. He didn't like the event or the choice of acts like Taylor Swift and Mumford & Sons. 'Those things are just not for me,' he told the BBC. 'It's a little bit corporate. The choice of artists they had on was awful. I thought it was very boring. I enjoyed the free alcohol, of course, but I thought the actual ceremony was boring. The party was brilliant, however. They could have had some brilliant people on. I'd have had on Noel Gallagher, you could have had The Stone Roses on. I don't need an award to inspire me to keep making music.' Which is fortunate, as Bugg lost out to Ben Howard.

Awards may not mean anything to Bugg, but hometown recognition certainly did. In February 2013, the line up for Nottingham's Splendour Festival was announced. The likes of Squeeze, KT Tunstall and Maximo Park were all on the bill – but it was the headline act that caught everyone's eye: Jake Bugg. Festival promoter George Akins says the announcement of Bugg as headliner was a key moment for the festival and for Nottingham: 'Splendour Festival is Nottingham's biggest music festival, so for him to headline that so quickly was amazing,' he told me. 'Jake started at The Courtyard Stage – which is the smallest stage for the local bands – and two years later he's headlining Splendour Festival on the main stage. It's just incredible.'

'It's just amazing what Jake's actually achieved over the last two years,' Jake's mum said on Radio 1. 'Starting off in his bedroom and then hearing that he's headlining Splendour, that he's playing some awesome festivals. I can't believe he's done so well. It's excellent.'

For George Akins, Bugg was becoming an inspirational figure to other musicians in Nottingham – Jake's success was proof that anyone could do it: 'I think, for all the local artists who are constantly gigging and plugging away, suddenly seeing a Nottingham artist headlining that quickly, I think has definitely given people a sense of... keep going, keep plugging away even when it's really tough, get there, it will happen. You definitely sense that – people have got hope now, that if they keep plugging away, they could get there.'

'It's a brilliant feeling,' Jake told *East Midlands Today*. 'Especially because two years ago I was opening the smaller stage. To be headlining this time round – it's a bit crazy. I'm just going to treat it like any other show and put the best performance in I can.'

Akins admits, though, that not everyone was completely convinced that Bugg was the right choice for top of the bill – some even thought they'd booked Bugg because he'd be less expensive. He went on to say, 'After we announced our Splendour bill, it was... What the fuck? Bit cheap, getting a guy from fucking Clifton to come down! That's what people thought, because our acts in the past had been multiple-album headliners rather than someone who's done one album. When we put Jake on, he'd only just gone to Number One in the album charts. Now the first week of someone going to Number One in the album charts, mainstream Nottingham don't know who he is. It takes them time to realise. But we were very confident – he was confident, his agent was confident. I don't think there was any question from our end that is was going to be a success but it took a while for people's perceptions to be changed about who he was, locally.'

Meanwhile, another single from the album was released: 'Seen It All'. In the video for the single, actor Michael Socha – another performer from Shane Meadows's *This Is England* stable – plays a partygoer who doesn't realise he's dead after an apparent stabbing. The video was directed by John Hardwick, making a return to promos after shooting the feature film *Svengali*, starring Martin Freeman and Vicky McClure, who'd played Jake's mum in the 'Two Fingers' video. It was shot in Glasgow while Bugg was on his first major headlining tour, and Jake only made a fleeting appearance, showing off his considerable table-tennis skills. The single only reached Number 61 in the charts – maybe people were happy with the album – but it was becoming apparent that singles weren't necessarily Bugg's forte.

But playing hometown gigs definitely was – and on his first major UK headlining tour in February he played Nottingham Rock City and became only the second local act to sell out the venue – the first being Dog Is Dead. His mum Leeysa was at the Rock City gig – chances to see her son at all were becoming few and far between: '[The] last time he was home before his Rock City show last night was a couple of weeks ago,' she told the *Nottingham Post*. 'But it was a flying visit on a Sunday afternoon. He'd just flown back from Vienna but then had to shoot off again to get ready for his UK tour. It was great to spend time together, as I know he's going to be so busy this year. He had his suitcase with him but, fortunately for me, he didn't ask me to wash anything as he was leaving for London the next morning. He brought me a rather nice bottle of my favourite Chanel perfume, although the best present for me is getting to see him, whenever his hectic schedule allows. It's natural for any parent to worry about their child growing up and flying the nest. Given the nature of his job, Jake is often thousands of miles away from home. Learning to let go has been tough for me at times. I miss him so much. However, I know he's got a great bunch of people around him, who have his best interests at heart. And we do talk on the phone regularly; at least a couple of times a week. He always makes time to get in touch, even when he's really busy. He's a good lad and he's very proud of where he comes from. That's why Nottingham features so heavily in many of his songs. He's so proud that the people of Nottingham support him the way they do.'

'He has complete cross-generational appeal,' says music journalist Mike Atkinson. 'When I went to see his sell-out show at Rock City, one of the notable things was the age range of the audience. You've got everyone from fourteen up to people in their sixties. You very rarely see that spread at a concert. In a way, he's got all those demographics that he can straddle.'

While Jake was in the city, he gave a tour of the area for DJ Zane Lowe for a Radio 1 documentary in the *Stories* series. He takes the DJ to Clifton and meets up with BBC Nottingham's Dean Jackson. Lowe does most of the talking as he is shown the sights but there is one telling moment that seemed to sum up Nottingham's attitude to Jake. Stopping off at a local chippy, Bugg asks for a sausage cob – the woman serving asks if he is, indeed, Jake Bugg. 'Yes, I am,' he says. 'You've done really well,' she tells him.

Nottingham wanted him to succeed – but not everyone was impressed by the documentary. Nottingham music journalist Mike Atkinson: 'It was an hour's worth of programme and in that time he didn't tip the nod to anyone within Nottingham that did help him with those early shows. I do wish that, having made it big, he would just tip a nod, just a nod to the community that helped him take those first steps. He made one disparaging reference to playing a shit gig at the Alley Café with a kind of, I won't be playing there again... and that disappoints me. Some of the other acts that are coming through are falling over themselves to say how amazing the music scene is but he never does. I'm sad about that.'

But music promoter George Akins believes that Bugg is giving back to Nottingham by providing proof that making it is not an unreasonable dream: 'The goals are there, the kids are seeing them now, they can touch them, they can feel them: that kid from Clifton did that. I think that's what's driving these kids on. It used to be like, Oh I want to be a musician... but I'm from Nottingham. No one makes it from Nottingham! Now they see the opportunities and they strive. The bands that used to be around didn't have to be that good, now they *have* to be good because the bar's been set and it drives them to be better bands and acts. Nottingham is a big city, half a million people, why have we never had a scene? It's not like we don't have enough people or enough talent. The talent's been here, they've just not been given the opportunity, I think. But we don't want to see this as just one act that came out of Nottingham – we want to see a scene. Jake stole the march, he's in the lead and I think everyone else is now going, "Right, that's the goal." The goal for these acts used to be, "Can I get a night at The Bodega?" Now it's, "I want to sell out Rock City."

On the tour, a strange phenomenon began to occur during Jake's performances – fighting among the crowd. An amped up, youthful audience plus alcohol plus Bugg's music seemed to trigger something in people. Bouncers were often called upon to eject troublesome gig-goers as the oikier elements of Bugg's audience settled their differences. It seemed to baffle Jake, especially when the fighting would start during slower songs like 'Somebody Told Me' – he would have to stop the show and confront the audience himself: 'What the fuck's going on?' he told them at a gig in Belfast. He seemed genuinely perplexed as to why his country twanging could provoke crowd violence. 'It's a ballad,' he told *Shortlist* magazine. 'Why start trouble to that? Although, to be fair, the other night in Leeds they were moshing at the end and about eight people got chucked out. Just because they could, basically. And in Newcastle we had about seven crowd surfers at once.'

While he was in Newcastle, Bugg was nearly on the receiving end of some argy-bargy himself. One of his support acts was girl rocker Findlay and she says she received a punch meant for Bugg after the show: 'We were having a late one up in Newcastle. The mini bar was getting hammered and it went on until 5am,' she told *The Sun*. 'An Irish girl was totally out of control. She'd had her arse out and everything. It kicked off and I got in the middle of it and took a punch for Jake. He owes me.'

Jake would notice a growing difference between the reaction he got in Britain to his live shows and the way audiences reacted in other countries: 'In America and Europe they come to see the music, they stand and watch the gig,' he said. 'It can be quite polite and quiet. Then there's us, who throw pints of piss and fists at each other. It was really strange after doing the UK tour, I loved it, then went to Sweden and everyone was really quiet. They're beautiful people though.'

Jake rounded off his tour with a gig at the Shepherd's Bush Empire on 28 February – his 19th birthday. It was a memorable show for lots of reasons: 'I remember calling him on his 19th birthday to wish him a happy birthday,' dad David later recalled. 'He'd just got off stage doing a gig and he was at party with Noel Gallagher, Paloma Faith, Jonathan Ross, Chris Evans... and I'd just got in from work.'

Reviewers were starting to fall over themselves to lay praise at Jake's door – and some of the reviews were starting to come from unexpected quarters. 'Walking out on stage to a scratchy old blues track was a clear nod to his retro musical tastes and influences – think Robert Johnson, Donovan, The Beatles, Jimi Hendrix and Nick Drake – but his music is thoroughly modern too (The Stone Roses and Arctic Monkeys are contemporary musical heroes),' wrote Fiona Raisbeck, reviewing the Shepherd's Bush gig. 'His faultless voice and song lyrics defy his age and life experiences as he switched back and forth between his up-tempo foot-stomping tracks such as "Taste It", "Two Fingers" and set closer "Lightning Bolt", and the softer finger-picking songs such as the beautiful "Simple As This", "Country Song" and "Broken". He barely speaks (bar a few mumbled song introductions and thank yous in his East Midlands drawl) and barely moves (other than to switch guitars between tracks), and he may be diminutive in stature, but he's completely captivating on stage for the duration of his set.' A typically strong review, you'd think – what's interesting about this one was the magazine it came from: women's magazine *Marie Claire*.

It was as clear a signal as possible that Bugg's profile was extending above and beyond the *NME* and the broadsheet rock journos. Jake's fame would take another step outside the accepted parameters when his name became linked with model Cara Delevingne. Jake had performed a short gig at fashion label Burberry's store in London's Regent Street – he'd come a long way from his tracksuit days on *This Is Live* in Nottingham. The gossip pages of the newspapers reported that Jake and Cara had left together after the show.

What gave the gossip an extra bit of frisson was Delevingne's background: she was posh... *really* posh. Her great-grandfather was a viscount, her grandfather is the former English Heritage chairman Sir Jocelyn Stevens, her godmother is actress Joan Collins and her mother's friendship with Sarah Ferguson – formerly married to Prince Andrew – meant she was childhood friends with Princesses Beatrice and Eugenie. All three went to the Frances Holland School for Girls near Sloane Square, then to the boarding school Bedales. She'd been signed by the Storm agency in 2009 aged 17 and had become the face of the Burberry brand in 2012. Vogue editor Alexandra Shulman had described her as, 'One of those girls who combine energy, wit, enthusiasm and the kind of edgy beauty that marks her out from the general pool of beautiful models.' She'd soon become a face about town in London, especially when it came to being snapped by the paparazzi with her friends Rihanna and Rita Ora.

This was a marriage made in tabloid heaven – to make it

even more appealing for the press, Cara had been previously linked to One Direction's Harry Styles – but some newspapers seemed genuinely shocked at the very possibility that Cara could be seeing Jake: SUPERMODEL CARA DELEVINGNE 'DATING TEENAGE MUSICIAN FROM COUNCIL ESTATE' WHO SHE MET AT RITA ORA PARTY, said the *Daily Mail*. *The Sun* was even more to the point: WHEN POSH TOTTY MEETS POP GROTTY, said the headline.

CARA BAGS BRITAIN'S COOLEST BOY, said *Grazia* magazine: 'They're in constant contact with one another and whenever they're in the same city, they try to meet up,' a 'source' told the paper. 'They both want to see if the relationship will develop. Cara is really into Jake and, though they're both very busy, they're trying to make it work.'

Jake seemed to have entered a very different world and would later confess to finding the attention 'intense'. 'It was weird,' he later told the *Daily Telegraph*. 'It was the first time I'd ever experienced anything like that. It's strange 'cause I knew, obviously, that people wanted to take photos of her, 'cause, you know, she's all over the world. But it was just confusing for me – what you gonna get out of getting a picture of me?'

But how would moving in such circles go down back in Nottingham? 'They are genuinely demographically worlds apart,' says *NUSIC*'s Mark Del. 'Jake is a working-class lad from a council estate – not the roughest by any means – and she's... well, there are many demographic runs between them. But I don't care.'

'I didn't care about our class difference,' Bugg confirmed when asked about the relationship by the paper that had run the 'Posh Totty' headline, *The Sun*. 'I don't care about class. I know I'm working class and I'm proud of that. I'll never judge anyone from where they are from, as long as they are a nice person. That is what matters.'

One thing that mattered a great deal to Jake was the unwanted attention the relationship generated: 'Round about that time there were reporters bothering me nana and granddad at their house, trying to get a story,' he later told *Q* magazine. 'That annoyed me as it had nothing to do with them.'

But as soon as it started, the relationship seemed to be over: 'Cara Delevingne has dumped singer Jake Bugg,' ran the story in the *Sunday People*. 'They had the potential to be the hottest couple in showbiz but the fever of romance has broken for Jake Bugg and Cara Delevingne. Supermodel Cara, 20, has dumped up-and-coming singer Jake after five months,' wrote the paper's Katie Hind. 'Both of their careers are starting to take off so it must have been hard for them to find time to spend together. But I gather Jake, 19, is devastated by the split. A source close to Cara told me, "Jake is very upset. Cara is a great catch and lots of fun. She definitely won't have any trouble finding a replacement for him." She briefly went out with One Direction heart-throb Harry Styles last year but it was rumoured bosses at her modelling agency, Storm, weren't bowled over by that and Cara gave him the elbow. Surely Jake couldn't have been bitten by the same Bugg? I reckon it's more likely it wasn't doing his street cred much good going out with someone so posh. After all, their backgrounds couldn't have been more different. Cara comes from a high-society aristocratic family and grew up in Belgravia. While Jake proudly hails from a council estate. Lovely while it lasted, guys.'

It appeared that Jake's flirtation with high society was over. But had it changed him? BBC Radio Nottingham's Dean Jackson offers this story: 'He'd been for a photo shoot some time ago and I saw some of the photos. I said, "Who took them?" And he said, "Oh, erm... [world famous photographer] David Bailey." You have to extract the information out of him – he's never name-dropped, he's never implied that he's left Nottingham behind – any of those things and he is exactly the same person today that he ever was.'

In his song 'Two Fingers', Jake described going back to Clifton to see his old friends. By now his world was very different to theirs and he admitted that it was getting harder for him to relate to their experiences: 'It is a bit strange, but I still speak to them,' he told *Q* magazine. 'I went back the other day and it's weird. I know Clifton better than anywhere but I've not been there for such a long time. I went to see my friends and my best mate was telling me he's now doing the night shift in Boots or whatever. It makes you feel a bit guilty in a way, but what can you do? If I do well enough, I can sort them out with a job in the future. They're very supportive of what I do. They could easily be bitter about it but they're not.'

CHAPTER THIRTEEN

HEROICALLY UN-ARSED

Soundtrack:
The Rolling Stones – 'Miss You' 1978
Johnny Cash – 'Hurt' 2002
KT Tunstall – 'Black Horse and the Cherry Tree' 2005

Major announcements with Jake's name attached to them were beginning to pile up by the spring of 2013. Jake was revealed as one of the supporting acts for The Rolling Stones at their Hyde Park gig in the summer. 'It's the biggest show I've played,' he said. 'Maybe not the most receptive crowd wise – you know seventy, eighty thousand people there to see The Rolling Stones, not Jake Bugg, but it's a complete honour.' Then he was nominated for an Ivor Novello Award for 'Two Fingers' and *GQ* magazine named him the 44th Best Dressed Man. The magazine went through a quick checklist to verify his cool credentials: 'Navy-blue Fred Perry Harrington zipped up to the chin? Check. Feet at ten to two? Check. Soul-stirring, Donovanesque vocals? Check. The ice-cool antidote to all those *X Factor* style rejects.'

Jake was also announced as one of the acts to appear on the main stage at Glastonbury – a considerable move up the running order from his appearance on the *Introducing* stage two years earlier. 'It's one of the biggest shows I've ever played in my life,' he told the *NME*, 'if not the biggest. I never know how it goes, it's up to the people who come along and listen to the tunes.'

Meanwhile, Jake's debut album was released in America, six months after it came out in the UK. For an album so steeped in Americana, the reaction from US critics promised to be interesting, and nothing represented the current state of the country's musical tastes quite like *Rolling Stone* magazine – reviewer Will Hermes gave it four stars out of five: 'Jake Bugg is a 19-year-old from a Nottingham housing project whose self-titled debut topped the UK pop charts late last year, somewhat astonishingly, with songs that seem steeped in albums such as *The Freewheelin' Bob Dylan*, *The "Chirping" Crickets* and *A Date With the Everly Brothers*. Alongside Mumford & Sons, Frank Turner and other back-to-basics Brits, Bugg is making artisanal folk rock with Whole Foods-scale ambition. On a table sagging with big-box pop, it's a small revelation. Essentially, Bugg does what countrywomen

Adele and Amy Winehouse did with soul: He yokes the spirit and styles of dated genres to the now.'

The *Los Angeles Times* had an interesting word to describe the album: 'bracing'. 'Accompanying himself on a guitar that probably cost ten quid, Bugg holds two fingers up to yesterday and moans about being stuck in Speed Bump City in scrappy early-rock ditties as full of Buddy Holly as they are of Bob Dylan.'

Filter magazine seemed to enjoy that fact that Bugg was a lippy Brit, with a few of the best American albums you can buy tucked under his arm: 'For a newcomer, British singer-songwriter Jake Bugg fires insults at his enemies like a wily veteran. But when you have the songs and fans (including the notoriously prickly Noel Gallagher) to back it up, there's not much your adversaries can do. With a twangy, piercing voice that's a cross between *Freewheelin'* Dylan and the Cash who conquered Folsom, the 19-year-old's sound combines retro folk with elements of Britpop that's as raw as it is original, which equals one of the more exciting debuts in some time.'

In another canny move by Bugg's team, 'Lightning Bolt' was used in an American commercial just prior to its release, in a similar way the track was used in the UK for Greene King IPA. In the US, though, the product was the soft drink Gatorade, though the way the track was used was very similar: yolking the past to represent a better version of the present. Here, we go back to 1965 – prime Bugg territory – to see the invention of Gatorade at the University of Florida for the Gators football team. Fast forward to today and we are offered the chance to 'Continue the Legend'.

To promote the album in America, Jake did the rounds of the US talk shows: David Letterman, Conan O'Brien and Ellen DeGeneres. It was a surreal sight: Bugg chatting to Ellen as the daytime audience stood on their feet to applaud him, buoyed by the knowledge that they were all getting a free copy of the album to take home. Ellen: 'What makes you love music so much?' Jake: 'I know that by listening to music it can make my day, so I want to make anyone else's day by playing it, yer know?'

Weird. But it did the trick. In the second week of April, *Jake Bugg* sold 6,000 copies in the US and entered the Billboard Top 100 at Number 75. It charted at Number 24 on the rock chart and Number 7 on the folk chart. And despite the fact that the album was still fresh onto the market, Jake revealed that work was underway on the follow-up. He'd even done some demos at the legendary Sun Studios in Memphis. 'I just stood there thinking: Johnny Cash has stood here and he did the same thing [as me],' Bugg later told *Rolling Stone* magazine. 'It's just mad.'

As the surroundings at Sun were so steeped in history it seemed sensible to see if any new material would be forth-coming. It was: 'It's a museum during the day and we booked a little session in the evening and rolled down with our guitars,' Jake later told XFM. 'From what I could see, Memphis is quite a poor area, people aren't living in the best of circumstances. But it was nice to have the bit of rock-and-roll history for me. It's a strange feeling to describe – I wrote two songs while I was there, they just came. I was with Iain at the time. They just came I didn't really try, or think, "Seeing as we're here we should try and write a song like this."'

While he was in Memphis, Jake also went to Graceland, the home of the late Elvis Presley: 'I didn't like being there,' he told the *NME*. 'Memphis is cool as fuck, but I felt like I was intruding on someone's property – I wouldn't like a load of people traipsing around my house with their dirty shoes.'

Jake also went to Clarksdale, Mississippi to 'The Crossroads' – an essential spot for any budding blues man. Legend has it that this was the spot where blues musician Robert Johnson made a deal with the Devil to sell his soul in exchange for the skills to master the art of the blues. 'They say he sold his soul at the crossroads,' Bugg said while visiting the spot. 'At the stroke of midnight the Devil came and tuned his guitar. He was one of the greatest players around.'

News about Jake's new album began to trickle out. Instead of the multiple producers involved on his debut, for the follow-up one producer would be dominating proceedings: Rick Rubin.

Rubin, the co-founder of Def Jam records, had worked with everyone from Adele to ZZ Top and had also forged a reputation for working with rap and metal acts as well as giving a fresh coat of credibility to classic artists. His work with Bugg hero Johnny Cash is largely credited with sealing

The Man in Black's reputation among a new generation of music fans and revitalising the country singer's career in the last decade of his life. Despite the Cash connection, Bugg would claim that he was unaware of Rubin's track record: 'When I first met Rick, I wasn't aware of all he had done and how well renowned he was but I think that helped and so I just cracked on and recorded my tunes,' he told the *NME*. 'The whole experience was inspiring. I learned a lot from Rick. I didn't know how well renowned he was when I went in there, so I kind of met the guy at face value and we got on really well. I also got the opportunity to work with some of the best players in the world, which has made me become much better as well. I've been listening to a lot of Neil Young and Nick Drake, and all that kind of stuff, and I think with these new songs you can kind of tell what I've been listening to. I still think it sounds like what I do. I want to emulate the first record – but better. A lot of people say he [Rubin] can be unorthodox but I've not experienced it yet. He's got this little ball he bounces up and down every now and again, but that's about it. There's nothing wrong with that.'

The album was recorded in two goes at Rubin's Shangri-La studios in Malibu. The former ranch house near Zuma Beach has a lot of history: it was built for actress and dancer Margo Albert and she named the house after the idyllic valley discovered by the characters in her best-known film *Lost Horizon* – the valley of Shangri-La. It's claimed the house – 25 miles from Los Angeles – had also been an upmarket brothel for the Hollywood elite before it became a recording studio in the early 1970s. The facility had a great deal of Bugg-friendly history too: Bob Dylan and The Band supervised its building and Dylan liked the site so much he lived in the garden for a while and his old tour bus is still there – it's now used as a playback suite so artists can listen to the recordings they've made. Shangri-La also featured in the Martin Scorsese documentary about The Band, *The Last Waltz*. It is, according to Adele, 'The coolest place on earth to record an album.'

It was Jake's management who had the idea of coupling him up with Rubin – not thinking for a moment that the producer would say yes. The first time he met Jake, Rubin thrust an acoustic guitar and told him to play him some tunes. Jake described the Shangri-La routine as, 'Wake up about noon, have a cup of coffee, then go in the studio, record two or three tracks a day, and embrace the night-time. The songs on the first album were written over a course of years, whereas these ones have all been written in the last year. Plus, they were all recorded by the same guy in the same place.' Two songs came quickly: 'Slumville Surprise' and a new version of 'Broken', featuring Chad Smith of the Red Hot Chili Peppers on drums. Typically, Jake was blissfully unaware of who the guest drummer was: 'Once he started playing I was very aware of how good he was,' he told told *Q* magazine. 'It was good though because it allowed me to get on with what I do. They played around me rather than me play around them. It's my record after all.'

'Since the band was already assembled, I asked Jake if he had any other songs written,' Rubin told US journalist Andrew Romano. 'He did and we started recording them. Each one was better than the one before, and I was wondering where these songs were coming from. His writing had a depth and maturity beyond his years.' As well as Chad Smith, Pete Thomas – who'd been a member of Elvis Costello's backing band The Attractions – was drafted in, as well as guitarist Matt Sweeney and bass player Jason Lader. 'Jake needed to be surrounded with great musicians who had the sensitivity to support what he plays in a natural musical way,' Rubin said. 'It's not as easy as it sounds.'

Rubin's choices of musicians to accompany Jake were in a different league to Bugg's live band, who had been left behind in England: 'As great players as they are, they haven't got the experience that the other guys have and that is one of the reasons that Rick brought them in,' Jake later explained to XFM. 'It was great for me, I learned a lot. It means I can musically direct my musicians better because I've seen how the more experienced ones do it – the top guys. But I think my live players are good musicians and they'll get there one day, they've just got a lot to learn still.'

Jake had gone to Shangri-La with the intention of completing just these two songs – in the end he decided to come back in August to finish the whole album. There was even talk of it being released before the end of 2013, barely a year after his debut: 'I don't really see any harm in it,' he told *Rolling Stone* when asked about this unusually fast turnaround. 'It seems like the right thing to do. Might as well keep up the momentum, you know?'

His first album was full of speed bumps, fat ones, stabbings and gangsters, the minutiae of Clifton life and the incessant ache to escape it. But now he had escaped it. He'd barely been in Nottingham since his success had kicked in and now he was in Malibu. He'd developed a taste for top-end guitars and had recently splashed out $20,000 on a 1954 Fender Telecaster in Nashville. There was a danger that album number two could be a series of songs about how awful it was being a successful musician, travelling the world, knocking around with supermodels and making lots of money. 'I want to give an insight to the same people who liked the first record about what my life is like now,' Jake told the *Daily Star*. 'That's not really a change from my first album, because all I'm doing is writing about my life. I'd never left Nottingham when I wrote those first songs but I've travelled the world and hopefully people can relate to what I've gone through. Whether people still like it is up to them but it'd be dishonest if I tried to write about life on a council estate again. All I can do is stick to describing what my life is like, same as before, and do it honestly.'

The Rubin version of 'Broken' – less subtle drums, more choir – was released as a single in June 2013. 'Mr Charisma delivers his most memorable song to date, with this re-recorded version of his album track "Broken",' said the *NME*. 'Producer Rick Rubin brings a sense of gravitas with a Guy Garveyesque choir and string section but, despite this, it all still feels a bit like music for a montage on BBC period drama *Call The Midwife*.'

'I was happy with the album version but I thought: If this is the last single before I put my debut to bed, I'd like to do something special,' Jake said. 'The choir and the strings on there are not genuine, they're samples or what not. So I wanted to do the same but with it being real and bring it to life a bit more and I think we've done that.'

The video to accompany 'Broken' – directed by photographer-turned-film-director Andrew Douglas – was shot in Hermitage, Tennessee. It sees Jake trying to soothe the redneck vibe in the Double E bar by singing the song on an open-mic night. The simple, atmospheric video and the Rubin magic still failed to achieve a genuine hit single for Jake – the song peaked at Number 44 in the UK charts. Singles weren't Bugg's thing, with or without Rick Rubin.

Jake was back in Britain that month for his return to Glastonbury. 2013 at Glastonbury was very much The Rolling Stones's year, with the veteran rockers still in the throes of their extended 50th-anniversary celebrations and marking the event by pummelling the opposition with a fearsome, hit-packed set. Despite so much attention on The Stones, Jake still managed to attract a few column inches with his set in front of a packed crowd. 'The cockiest Lonnie Donegan wannabe in Nottingham tears up the roots of rock'n'roll by making like a Sun Records bluegrass balladeer appealing against an Asbo,' said *The Guardian*. 'Switching between urgent skiffle, antique troubadour turns and a cover of Neil Young's "Hey Hey, My My", Bugg gazes nonchalantly over a headliner-level crowd and sets about justifying his position at the forefront of the pre-rock revival by contemporising his rootsy attack with tales from tearaway Britain.'

For some reviewers, the scale of the event was a bit too much for Bugg's sparse sound: 'By the time man of the moment Jake Bugg took to the Pyramid Stage the crowd stretched all the way up the hill to the camping grounds,' said *The Independent*. 'A mass of humanity punctuated by banners and flags; smiley faces, skull and crossbones and various international flags, the massive crowd was probably the biggest Bugg has played [to]. On the one hand, it's great to see a home-grown singer-songwriter take to the main stage, but personally his ballads seem to fall a little flat in such a large arena. The crowd's polite applause seems to agree.'

'Despite a heaving early-afternoon slot on the Pyramid stage, the heroically un-arsed Bugg constantly looks like you're taking slightly too much time ahead of him at the supermarket checkout,' said the *NME*. 'But that deadpan scowl is balanced out with new songs, one a chomping-at-the-bit country rocker called "Slumville Surprise".'

One incident at Glastonbury would serve to remind Jake of how far he'd come: 'In the crowd there was a girl on some lad's shoulders that I went to school with for years,' he told *The Guardian*. 'And she always said to me, "I'll never get your music – why do you listen to that crap?" And she was singing all the words to the songs. That was mad.'

Even madder was what happened when Jake played at a smaller acoustic show away from the main stage: 'I saw a lot of people start looking at this woman,' he told *Spotify*. 'Then this guy stood up and she hugged him and he proposed to her. He asked her to marry him in the middle of my song. So halfway through the song I said congratulations. That's very nice but, if I were going to propose, I wouldn't do it at a Jake Bugg gig.'

Through June and into July, Bugg had worked his way across Europe, with dates in Mallorca, Nuremberg, Sweden, Luxembourg, France, Portugal and Denmark. On 13 July he hit London for his support slot with The Rolling Stones. But as far as Nottingham was concerned, this was all just a warm-up for the big one: Splendour. For George Akins, the man behind the festival, taking a chance on making Jake the headliner had paid off: 'There'd been a bit of a backlash on the Internet initially,' Akins told me. 'It was like, What the fuck is this? Then he shut them all up when he sold more tickets than anyone else did. It was a vindication really for us booking him. We never would have believed six years ago when we started doing Splendour that this would ever happen, it's a real surprise. I hope that part of what we've done is part of the reason that something's happening in Nottingham at the moment. I hope we're part of that, I feel we're part of that.'

From Jake's point of view, the pressure was on: 'It'll be the first festival I've headlined so it's a massive thing for me,' he told journalist Simon Wilson. 'But as much as I'm looking forward to it and excited about being the headline act, I've got to treat it like any other gig and play the way I play. I've got to give it a hundred per cent, stay focused and try to give the folks a good show.'

Nottingham was now existing in a post-Bugg world. His success had changed the city, the music scene and the way Nottingham viewed itself. Splendour 2013 was the first opportunity to celebrate the fact. Established acts like Squeeze, Maximo Park and KT Tunstall seemed heavily outnumbered – local acts were everywhere: Dog Is Dead, Indiana, Harleighbleu, Sam Jones, Kagoule, Injured Birds, Saint Raymond, Georgie Rose and the fabulously named The Gorgeous Chans.

The *Nottingham Post* could be forgiven for crowing that this was 'the year our music came of age'.

NUSIC's Mark Del was on hand to introduce Jake on stage that day but organisers had laid on a surprise: 'I said, "Tonight, Nottingham, Jake comes home,"' recalls Del. 'That cued a film that had been made by Notts TV that showed Jake walking from Clifton with his guitar and getting closer and closer and closer – all in black-and-white. Then it cut to Jake backstage, turned into colour and Jake walked out on stage. Jake's a man of few words, so he let the intro do the talking. I think a lot of people were caught up in the significance of it.'

Promoter George Akins: 'It was great progression – we end up with this great Nottingham scene on this great bill. We sold a lot of tickets and Jake was triumphant really at the end. It was just a wonderful, wonderful conclusion to his rise from Clifton to headlining Splendour. I think the video running up to him coming on stage – walking from Clifton all the way to Splendour – told a fantastic story really.'

Mark Del: 'It was amazing. It was 20,000 Nottingham music lovers singing along to a Nottingham Number One – how could you not feel that was a pretty special moment? Particularly "Broken", when everyone was singing the words back – that felt like a moment. It was different to any other head-liner that walked on stage. This is a kid living his dream – a kid from down the road. You could hear it in the crowd... "I used to know his mum's hairdresser" – all those local connections. There was a significant part of the crowd that felt they had a connection to the artist. There was a feeling of mass connection that you can only get at a local event. There was a symbolism of how the Nottingham music scene has come of age. It felt like the crowd was aware that this was a significant moment for Nottingham as well as the artist. It was the icing on the cake for the most Notts-tastic Splendour ever: 15 Nottingham artists in all. To use a footballing analogy, it's like winning the league with home-grown players when your striker was born five miles down the road and your goalkeeper was born two miles down the road.'

There was only one review that mattered that day and, as ever, it was fantastically partisan: 'Performing his first ever festival headline set, Jake Bugg took the packed hill in his stride, unfazed as ever by his mushrooming success,' went the write up in the *Nottingham Post*. 'Well, when you've just played the Pyramid Stage at Glastonbury and supported The Rolling Stones at Hyde Park, what fear could Splendour possibly hold? It was all a far cry from his bottom-of-the-bill appearance at The Courtyard Stage two years ago. Jake's triumph set the seal on a landmark event for Nottingham music. This was a public celebration of our scene's coming of age, drawing on genres across the musical spectrum and demonstrating just how far we have progressed in recent years. Where Jake Bugg and Dog Is Dead have led, others are certain to follow. Next year, will there even be space for out-of-town acts? We can but dream!'

When the Splendour show was over, it was a chance for a get-together for Jake's family and friends: 'I was at Jake's Splendour aftershow party,' *NUSIC*'s Mark Del told me. 'Jason [Hart] was there and Jason's family were there, his girlfriend, his aunt and uncle. There was clearly a very strong bond between the two families. It was like the Hart family and the Bugg family were having a wedding! It really struck me that there's a really strong bond here. When you're friends with people's aunts and uncles, it's gone beyond the normal artist/manager relationship.'

CHAPTER FOURTEEN

THIS IS FUCKING REAL!

Soundtrack:
The Stooges – 'I Wanna Be Your Dog' 1969
Rocket From The Crypt – 'On A Rope' 1995
Arctic Monkeys – 'Nettles' 2007

Jake went from the Splendour Festival in Nottingham to the Splendour in the Grass Festival in Sydney, Australia. His no-nonsense style seemed tailor-made for an Aussie audience and to build up the buzz he played a 'secret' gig – heavily touted on social media beforehand – at the city's Rocks Square.

At the Splendour in the Grass Festival itself, Jake was mid-table on the second day – his old pals Mumford & Sons had headlined the day before – but as far as some reviewers were concerned, he was the standout act: 'It could have been the earlier time slot allowing natural sunlight to be injected into the tent, but Jake's stage set-up was devoid of fancy lighting displays and effects, which meant there was nothing there to distract from the star's killer vocals,' said MTV Australia. 'Regularly switching between electric and acoustic guitars throughout the show, Bugg managed to keep the crowd in full swing by mixing up the energy between tracks. A powerful acoustic performance of "Broken" left the audience in complete awe of the star's undeniable natural talent. Bugg's entire performance had the crowd kicking up their muddy gumboot-clad heels and moving to the beat like a good old-fashioned hoedown. Undoubtedly one of the most powerful and moving sets of Splendour thus far.'

Shows in Canada, Tokyo, Austria, The Netherlands and Northern Ireland followed before he headed back to Malibu and Rick Rubin's studio specifically to finish recording his second album. He spent two weeks recording the remaining tracks that would complete it. He lived at the studio too and this would be the longest period of time that he'd stay in one place since his career kicked in. One song that stood out during the sessions was called 'Pretty Lady'. The lyrics seemed to indicate the song was about his difficult relationship with model Cara Delevingne – a romance seemingly ruined by the level of attention that the couple generated. 'People were making stories up about it,' Jake told journalist Simon Goddard. 'So I made my own from it.' As recording came to an end in the first week of September, it was decided to drop the song from the album's running order. 'Not because of the subject,' he later claimed, 'but when the final mixes came back, it was one of them [songs] that didn't seem so strong. I wanted "Pretty Lady" on there – I find it hard to talk about some of these songs because I'm not someone who really expresses how I'm feeling. Which is probably why everyone thinks I'm such a moody dickhead. But there are cases where you write songs because you didn't want to speak about the subject. If I could talk about them, I would, but I write songs instead. So people can say what they want about that song. And it will come out as a B-side or something. I'm not scared of putting that out into the world. We all have things that we might not wanna speak about but I think it's good for my soul to get it out there.'

Jake liked the surroundings of Rick Rubin's studio so much that he told one journalist that he didn't want to leave – but the work rate was considerable and many tracks were banged down live: 'I think you capture a bit of magic doing that, something you can't explain,' Bugg told Radio 1. 'It came quick but, for me, music's what I do to get away from stuff... Even though it's been crazy, when I have time to myself, it's me picking up my guitar... I travelled lots and had some crazy experiences, so I had a lot to write about!'

While Jake was putting the finishing touches to the album, he was the subject of fairly unusual discussion back in Nottingham. During a speech at the city's university, none other than Mark Carney, the Governor of the Bank of

England, had decided to show off his local knowledge and his indie credentials by dropping Bugg's name into a speech on UK productivity. 'The UK is no more productive than it was back in 2005,' Carney told his audience. 'And to put it in context, that was before Nottingham's own Jake Bugg got his first guitar and since then, as you know, he's had a Number One record and a string of very successful gigs. He's become a lot more productive, and the critical question is how much more, and how quickly can productivity improve across the broader economy.'

'Why'd he have to drag me into it?' was Bugg's response when asked about Carney's comments while recording in Malibu. There's a long and inglorious tradition of people in public life claiming hip credentials by name-checking modern acts – former prime minister Gordon Brown once looked an interviewer in the eye and said he liked the Arctic Monkeys – and Carney seemed worried he'd fallen into the same trap: 'I hope I haven't jinxed it but I saw him play in Hyde Park and he was outstanding,' explained Carney when asked about his shout-out on *CITY A.M.* website.

The first indication of Jake's productivity came via the news that Shane Meadows – the man behind the *This Is England* films that had provided something of a repertory company for Jake's videos – would be directing the video for Bugg's new single. Meadows – born in Staffordshire but an honorary Nottingham lad after moving to the city aged 20 – had long been noted for his musical connections and credentials: he'd directed The Stone Roses documentary

Made of Stone and had talked the aforementioned Arctic Monkeys into appearing in his spoof rockumentary *Le Donk & Scor-zay-zee*. The filming that Meadows did turned out to be for Bugg's second single.

On 23 September all was revealed. The first single was to be 'What Doesn't Kill You', and the album it would be taken from would be named after Rubin's studio: *Shangri La*. Amazingly, the album would be released 13 months after its predecessor. Easy, claimed Bugg – if you pull your finger out. 'There are some artists out there that could do it,' Bugg told website *Manchester Confidential*, 'but they decide to milk a record for a few years, then there are some who couldn't put a record out every year, they haven't got it in them. Whenever the record is ready, that's when it should be released. Put it out there. You shouldn't sit on a record if it's ready.'

'What Doesn't Kill You' was a sonic feint that took most reviewers and fans by surprise. No boom-chikka-boom country twang here – the song was a 124-second garage-rock banger. Arctic Monkeys were the obvious touchstone – old Monkeys B-side 'Nettles' was in there somewhere – but older heads could point to 'On A Rope' by Rocket From the Crypt, as well 'I Wanna Be Your Dog' by The Stooges. Those expecting lyrics about hotel rooms, supermodels and Malibu were disappointed: we're back on the Clifton estate with late nights, beatings and robbings. Jake played the guitar solos on the song, despite the presence of some heavyweight guitarists in the studio. 'I was working on another song but it just wasn't going anywhere,' Jake told XFM when he was asked about the song. 'I got distracted and started playing these other chords instead – it came completely by accident. It's about wherever you go in the world you want to avoid confrontation. It's kind of the reason why I left where I was from, but sometimes you can't avoid it. It's one of those songs that came very quickly really. I suppose it was exaggerated slightly, it was based on a friend who got in a fight one night, got a big moral about the story. It's not just about a fight, it can be about many things as well, which is probably why I expanded the meaning of it.'

When the video was released many journalists assumed it was Shane Meadows's work – in fact this was director Andrew Douglas on duty once again to direct the video to accompany the single and he clearly understood the musical references that the song was making, as well as Bugg's predilection for doing it in one take: 'This song yelled rock'n'roll in all its raw simplicity,' Douglas told *Promo News*. 'It seemed to connect to an earlier period of music, like the Velvets or The Stooges, and we tried to reflect that raw direct feel in the simplicity of the shoot. One camera, four takes, and a simple but intense performance from Jake.' The film was given a grainy, documentary look, the idea being, 'to connect Jake to the rootsy, unaffected feel of Cash or Dylan.'

The video is Jake, plus leather jacket, plus Stratocaster guitar, plus amp and nothing more – apart from off screen encouragement, reminding and encouraging Bugg that this is 'not a fucking game, Jake... This is fucking real!' Bugg barely gives a glance to the camera and two minutes later it's all over.

Released on 24 September, the single attracted fairly equal portions of puzzlement and praise. 'Now he's got us primed for tales of travelling the world with his hero Noel Gallagher, recording with legends like Rick Rubin and hooking up with Cara Delevingne, but here's Jake singing about feeling like you're up against the world, still eschewing the glitz and the glamour in favour of his council-estate grit,' said the *NME*. '[He is] reinstating himself as the grand observer of life's darker moments that made up most of his self-titled debut.'

But not everyone was quite as on-message as the *NME*: 'Jake Bugg's gone electric with new single "What Doesn't Kill You", and the end results aren't very promising,' said entertainment website *Crave*. 'The 19-year-old singer-songwriter burst onto the scene last year with his eponymous debut album, which shot straight to Number One in the album charts. Now he has announced the upcoming release of his follow-up LP, *Shangri La*, along with unveiling its first single, which unfortunately sounds more like The View than Bob Dylan.'

In America – where Bugg's managers surely had their sights set – the reaction was more positive: 'Jake Bugg has the songwriting chops to pivot towards the mainstream rock scene in the United States,' said *Billboard* magazine. 'But the 19-year-old has instead chosen to lead his sophomore album *Shangri La* with a pissed-off wiry whirl that just barely crosses the two-minute mark. "What Doesn't Kill You" evokes the angular punk of the mid-2000s, with Bugg packaging his tales of woe in slippery verses and letting his wounds fester during a searingly bluesy electric solo.'

What was more surprising than the critics' reactions were those of Bugg's fans. His Facebook page was soon filled with reactions to the single… and many weren't on board with the punkier sound of 'What Doesn't Kill You': 'Honestly it is horrible,' said one fan. 'This is what happens when Rick Rubin gets hold of your record. Maybe you didn't have the nerve to tell Rick it wasn't working for you? Or maybe you are still a lot star-struck. How disappointing.' Another posted: 'Oh Jake!!?? You're not in the Arctic Monkeys mate!! Stick to the acoustic stuff! It's wot u do best!' It wasn't all bad though and at least some of Jake's fans knew enough about musical history to flag up a precedent: 'The negative comments remind me of the reactions Dylan got when he went electric.'

Despite the heavy backing of Radio 1 – especially Zane Lowe – the single only grazed the charts, peaking at Number 44. But critical success easily outweighed sales of his singles. His debut album was shortlisted for the Mercury Prize – and much was made of the age difference between Bugg and one of the other nominees, 66-year-old David Bowie. 'There's an engaging rockabilly intensity to Jake Bugg's catchy folk rants, his simple strum'n'drum arrangements allowing that sharp, piercing voice to cut through unhindered on songs such as the single "Lightning Bolt",' said *The Independent*, assessing Jake's chances of winning. 'Bugg's is a gritty, urban-realist form of folk music, depicting with premature world-weariness a youth culture pockmarked by booze, drug abuse and routine violence. But it's balanced by a consolatory tenderness that's entirely in keeping with his bohemian skiffle style.'

Bugg himself was characteristically nonplussed about the nomination: 'That's not why I make music, to get awards,' he told the *Nottingham Post*. 'It's great to be nominated but the Mercurys don't mean a whole lot to me.'

Jake was also in the running for Best New Act in the Q Awards. His chief competition there was Tom Odell. In some quarters, Odell was seen as the anti-Bugg contender. Although Odell had started at open-mic nights, just like Jake, he was seen as 'posh' – he'd been born in Chichester and went to the £20,000-a-year Seaford School in East Sussex. For some, Odell's softy credentials were set in stone when his dad rang the *NME* to complain about a bad review of his son's debut album *Long Way Down* – to be fair to Odell senior, the paper had described Odell's music as 'musical syphilis' and said that the young musician was a 'poor, misguided wannabe who's fallen into the hands of the music-industry equivalent of Hungarian sex traffickers.'

There was much talk of Bugg and Odell 'fighting it out' for the prize but the pair had toured together and Odell seemed to sense a kinship with Bugg: they were of a similar age and were both victims of serial pigeonholing by the press: 'Everyone desperately tries to find a sound and to pin you to a sound, like Jake Bugg,' Odell said. 'They say he sounds like Bob Dylan or Oasis... You can't be a new artist and just be yourself. I mean, I have a whole load of different influences that I don't... There's not just one artist... I mean, I really want to be something that someone hasn't heard before.'

In the end, Jake lost out to James Blake for the Mercury but, in true Bugg style, he had a pop at both Blake and the awards afterwards: 'I didn't particularly enjoy his performance at the Mercury Awards,' he told the BBC, 'but I could see that he's talented. I was quite pleased that I didn't win the Mercury because I was quite drunk and I didn't want to go on that stage and make a speech, to be honest.'

He did, however, win the *Q* Award for Best New Act and made the shortest ever acceptance speech: 'Cheers,' he said before walking off the stage.

The follow-up to 'What Doesn't Kill You' came in October, with another rockabilly stomper, 'Slumville Sunrise'. The hush-hush video that Bugg had shot with Shane Meadows was finally revealed and what a change it was from the usual Jake moodiethons. In a short film that's nearly three times the length of the song, Bugg plays 'Jake', a shell-suited chancer out to steal an engagement ring for his girlfriend, played by Rosamund Hanson from, you guessed it, *This Is England*. For the purposes of the video, he's wearing a tracksuit that rivalled – but not surpassed – the one he wore back in the day in the *This Is Live* video. 'We wanted to pick the most awful tracksuit we could find,' Meadows told the *NME*, 'something he just wouldn't want to wear.'

Bugg leads assorted jewellers, police officers, grannies, Elvis impersonators and Shane Meadows himself on a Benny Hill-style chase through the choicer areas of Nottingham, including Sneinton, the watersports centre at Holme Pierrepont and the notorious St Ann's area. 'It was a fun day shooting that,' he told the *Nottingham Post*. 'I was in Malibu finishing the album the day before. Coming back brought me back to reality. Although I was robbing a jewellery store in a shell suit with old ladies running after me, which I'd never done before. It was funny, man. I haven't had that much fun for a while.'

It's a deliberately cheesy affair – much of it shot against a green screen in the style of 'Is This The Way To Amarrilo'. Meadows had made videos previously for Richard Hawley, former band mate of Bugg co-songwriter Crispin Hunt. He'd agreed to come out of 'retirement' because Bugg had done him a favour: 'It was nice to do one again,' he said. 'It was an honour to do it for Jake – I owed him big-time for playing at my 40th last year. I had a great laugh making it. It was the best craic I've had in ages.'

The chase ends with Bugg presenting the ring to a heavily pregnant Hanson in an improvised scene that reveals the normally monosyllabic Jake to be quite the actor: 'It wasn't scripted, no,' Bugg later told BBC Nottingham's Dean Jackson. 'That was the first thing we did for the video – the very first thing. I'm in this room, I don't know what I'm doing. Shane's saying, "You've robbed this ring, blah, blah, blah." It was just improvisation really, being an exaggerated version of yourself. I quite like the idea of being in a position where you don't have to be yourself. It's another way of expressing how you're feeling. It's a creative thing – and it puts you on the spot as well, it makes you have to think of things quite quick.'

The sound of the song was simple with the words spat out like a rockabilly rap – in lyrical terms, Jake was still in Clifton, dreaming of escape for 'Slumville Sunrise'. 'It's funny how I didn't think I was going to be talking about life back home and stuff like that after so much had changed,' he told XFM. 'But it was quite interesting after everything that had happened to go back and see things from a completely different perspective. It was something that inspired me quite a bit.'

Reviews were mixed, with many journalists still looking for clues as to how the track would point to Jake's second album. Jake did the promo rounds, including a return to Jools Holland's *Later* studios. Even the normally loyal *NME* wasn't fully on board: 'A friend described last week's *Later… With Jools Holland* performance as "Like watching George Formby murdering an Arctic Monkeys B-side." Harsh maybe, but not inaccurate. What rescues "Slumville Sunrise" is Bugg's gritty charm and endearing dedication to make sure you feel the song, straining on every line like he's gasping for air. It's quick, catchy and the Shane Meadows-directed video will make it even more memorable.'

'With a fun tongue-in-cheek video, Jake Bugg actually releases one of his best songs since "Lighting Bolt",' said music website *All-Noise* in a cautious seven-out-of-ten review. 'I have a love-hate relationship with Bugg: everyone seems to love him, I'm not a big fan, but "Slumville Sunrise", with its Arctic Monkeys sound and driving guitar is a much better song than we've had from him for a long time, and might just win over some people like me who haven't enjoyed some of his other numbers.'

'A rockabilly burner from the new sheriff of Nottingham about a long, painful night in a town he loathes,' said *Rolling Stone*, giving the American take on the single. 'Yet he still makes it sound like a victory.'

The single was 'A-listed' by Radio 1 and Radio 6 Music – it was played all the time in straightforward terms – yet still failed to make a big impression on the charts. BBC Nottingham's Dean Jackson has a theory about why these singles didn't quite hit home: 'Everyone knew the album would drop very soon so there was no harm hanging on a couple of weeks to get the full package – whereas with the first album, the release date wasn't known till well after "Lightning Bolt" and "Two Fingers" had been kicking around for a while.'

But the real battle was still to come – with a UK tour lined up and a release date of 18 November for his new album, Bugg had a lot to prove. Could he turn out a viable second album 13 months after his first? And in terms of credibility, had he left the Clifton Boulevard far behind? Had his head been turned by supermodels, money and Malibu? 'I will never forget where I'm from,' he insisted. 'It's made me into who I am. I was there [in Clifton] for 17 years, all my life. I knew there was a world out there, I wanted to see it and I'm getting to do that. It's the people I miss. When I get back to Clifton, you do go to places and they do hold memories but I spent so much time there that I wanted to see the rest of the world.'

CHAPTER FIFTEEN

1,000

Soundtrack:
Glen Campbell – 'By The Time I Get To Phoenix' 1968
Elvis Costello and The Attractions – '(I Don't Want To Go To) Chelsea' 1978
Bruce Springsteen – 'I'm On Fire' 1985

Perhaps Jake was loosening up a little as his twentieth birthday approached but he managed a whole two sentences in the 'thank you' section of his second album *Shangri La*. The sentiment was largely the same – an appreciation of those who have assisted thus far – but the slight expansion was a signal of more ambitious things to come.

As well as Bugg and Iain Archer, two new names were to be found on the writers' credits this time round. Despite a prolific solo career and critical plaudits aplenty, Nashville-based musician Brendan Benson is probably best known outside of muso circles for his work with Jack White in The Raconteurs. The Bugg/Benson connection had been suggested by Jake's publishing company. 'I went down to Nashville on a little trip with Iain [Archer],' Jake told *Spin* magazine. 'I was very sceptical about it: three blokes in a room with guitars. I was like, Well, how on earth is this going to work? But we started jamming around, and I shared a few riffs I had. It was cool. When I'm working with people, I never want to feel like the task is to write a song. It's all just jamming around, like people used to do back in the day.'

Matt Sweeney is another US musician who is better known to other musicians than he is to the wider public. He's worked with the right kind of musicians, from Bonnie 'Prince' Billy to Billy Corgan, but the fact that he played on Johnny Cash's posthumous album *American V: A Hundred Highways* must have resonated with Bugg. And make no mistake – *Shangri La* is an American album.

If *Jake Bugg* was an album of the 1950s and 1960s, then *Shangri La* belongs in the early 1970s, the soundtrack to a road movie like *Vanishing Point* or *Electra Glide in Blue*. It invokes The Stooges, Glenn Campbell, John Denver, and Simon and Garfunkel more than Buddy Holly or Johnny Cash. Actually, the first track, 'There's A Beast And We All Feed It' invokes none other than Jake Bugg – as a song, it's a close cousin to 'Trouble Town' and has a lyrical rhythm akin to Bob Dylan's 'Subterranean Homesick Blues'. You're immediately on familiar ground and it's unlikely to scare you off early doors. It's a song about negativity – get hold of something nice? Someone will probably want to ruin it for you, possibly someone from the music industry. 'This was written in the Sun Studios,' Jake later said. 'The beast can be any industry – I'm sure a lot of the same things happen in all kinds of areas of business.'

With 'There's A Beast And We All Feed It', Bugg utilised a classic council estate fighting technique – get the first punch in and make sure it's an aggressive one. He's having a pop at the machinations of the music industry and the needs of the publicity machine that surrounds and supports it: 'That's just being a part of the mechanical machine in any industry,' he explained to journalist Ari Lipsitz. 'Sometimes you don't want to help the machine to carry on existing – but despite whether we want to or not, we can't help but encourage it and give it something to feed on.'

Next up are the singles – the bangers are up front on this album – and 'Slumville Surprise' and 'What Doesn't Kill You' mean that we are less than seven minutes into the album and three tracks have already whizzed by. Perhaps these punk rock stompers are there to remind people that this is an album by a teenager – and teenagers are more than within their rights to be making a racket.

Once that point is made, 'Me And You' comes along, an acoustic shuffle that is one of the tracks on the album written solely by Jake – yet there's a good case to be made for it being the best track here. Tellingly, it's the first song here about Bugg's post-Clifton life. It's not Clifton he's trying to escape, it's the intrusive world of fame. The song is a countrified sibling of Bruce Springsteen's 'I'm On Fire', and it could well be about his relationship with Cara Delevingne. It's Jake and his gal against the world – being followed, cameras flashing – but believing that they can make it if only they were left alone. The uncharacteristically gentle drums are played by Chad Smith of Red Hot Chili Peppers: 'You can't tell it's him,' Jake told DJ John Kennedy. 'He's not doing his funky drumming and it's nice when he gets on the brushes. This started when I was on the tour bus, just a few traditional chords and I kept saying the words "Me and you". And I thought… that's quite nice, that could mean a lot for many people.'

From a track written by Jake on his own to a three-hander – 'Messed Up Kids' is credited to Bugg/Benson/Archer and, despite being the most American sounding, commercial track on the album, lyrically it's a return to a grimmer, bleaker version of Clifton. This one is a hopeless world of dealers, breeze blocks and prostitutes. The track is downbeat even by Jake's standards and it's unlikely to be used by the Clifton Tourist Board any time soon.

'A Song About Love' is Glenn Campbell meets Oasis; it's akin to the widescreen ballads that songwriter Jimmy Webb wrote for Campbell and others in the late 1960s and early 1970s. It's intimate yet big at the same time and feels like a standard rather than a new track. Pete Thomas of The Attractions plays drums here and there are some tricky time changes that Bugg was under pressure to change from his co-writers: 'They were like, It needs to be 4/4, it needs to be straight, it's a ballad. I'm like, No, I'm not doing that, it's my song – it's just going to take the emotion away. We recorded it and they said, "You were right to stick to your guns." I'm like, course, it's my song – I'm not going to change it for anyone. That's how I play it and that's how it's going to be.'

'All Your Reasons' is the second Bugg solo track here – again we're in the early 1970s with some slinky guitar playing from Matt Sweeney: 'Some of the best guitar playing I've heard recently,' Jake said. 'I was just grateful that it was on my track.' Bugg was clearly taken with the laid-back guitarist and he even appeared on Sweeney's YouTube show *Guitar Moves*, showing the older musician his growing mastery of blues, country and flamenco guitar techniques. As well as some great guitar playing, 'All Your Reasons' has a surprisingly dour lyric that's weaved through with disappointment, apology and regret. Not what you'd expect from a 19-year-old with the world at his feet. It's like the late English singer-songwriter Nick Drake has gone electric – very American yet quite English at the same time.

The life and times of a drug dealer is the theme of 'Kingpin', with Bugg inhabiting the character of a lowlife in the way that Johnny Cash used to do. Written in Nashville, Bugg is channelling 1970s pub rockers Doctor Feelgood here and it's not a sound that's been referenced for a very long time.

'Kitchen Table' is the track that was included on *Shangri*

La in favour of 'Pretty Lady'. If there's a song that you are immediately reminded of here, it's 'Woodstock' by Joni Mitchell, particularly the 1970 cover version by Matthews' Southern Comfort. It's all late-night electric piano and rimshot drums and the other touchstone here is the late British folk musician John Martyn, particularly the spacey, organic feel of his 'Solid Air' album. Here, Bugg is recounting a doomed relationship with an older woman. 'It's about when I got signed,' he later explained. 'I was in a relationship with somebody – not a particularly nice person – and she'd come in and she'd say, "Oh, what song are you playing there? That's a nice song." But it was about wanting to leave this person behind. I was in very deep and found it quite difficult at the time because she was much older than I was. But, you know, I got a song out of it.'

'Pine Trees' – or 'Paaarn Trees' as it comes out here in Bugg's inimitable East Midlands modulation – evokes the low-key acoustica of the debut album. It's a Jake escape song but it's not Clifton he's trying to get away from this time, it's compromise and doing what's expected of you.

'Simple Pleasures' gets guitarist Matt Sweeney a songwriting credit. It has a 1990s post-grunge feel about it – Sweeney has played with US acts like Guided By Voices – with a quiet/loud/quiet dynamic.

Finally, there's 'Storm Passes Away', a country strum-a-long that would sit happily on Bugg's first album – apart from the fact that this one was written in Nashville, not Clifton. You imagine him singing it on *This Is Live* back in the day. It's fine but it's filler – even Bugg himself seems to acknowledge as much: 'This song out of all the other songs is probably the least relevant to me but it's a nice one to end with, because it might be one of these songs that becomes relevant one day and the next day not so much. It's all about how you think of it, how you picture it. I thought it was a good one to end with. Just a little country song.'

That aside, with the range of tones, sounds and moods available on *Shangri La*, the level of playing and the quality of the songs, there's a straightforward question to be asked about the album: is it as good as his debut effort? There is a very good case to be made that *Shangri La* is better than Bugg's first album on almost every level.

Reviewers were, frankly, a little puzzled – even the slavishly loyal *NME* was cautious to the point of being damning: 'A cynic might suggest that the swift turnaround between Jake Bugg's first album and its follow-up owes less to the way Dylan and Donovan used to churn them out, and more to Bugg's dwindling proximity to his favourite subject, the mean crescents of Clifton,' said reviewer Barry Nicolson, giving the album a watery six out of ten. 'That cynic may just be onto something too – leave it any longer, be photographed on the arm of another London socialite, and kitchen-sink shanties like "Slumville Sunrise" or "Messed Up Kids" might start to sound as inauthentic as the talent show wannabes he has a habit of turning his ire towards. Forgetting where you came from is one thing, but pretending it's still where you're at can be just as foolish. By rush-releasing *Shangri La*, Bugg manages to circumvent some second-album pratfalls, although he's succumbed to the most obvious one – it's not as good as his first. That's despite the efforts of Rick Rubin, whose presence is a much bigger deal in theory than in practice. Bugg claims to have been unaware of the producer's reputation before they began working together, and the biggest change Rubin presides over is a slight shift into rockier territory, musically and figuratively. Bugg's voice – an acquired taste at the best of times – simply isn't suited to the nuance-free likes of "What Doesn't Kill You" or "Kingpin", honking and braying his way through both like a man having his backside paddled with a splintery cricket bat.'

The *Observer* seemed equally hung up about Jake's delivery – his Midlands twang seemingly a problem for southern critics: 'Bugg's second album opens with the kind of high-speed wordiness and skiffley jangle that he does best – scrappy and audibly northern throwback rock that splits the difference between Arctic Monkeys and Oasis,' wrote Hermione Hoby. 'But this is not always a wholly good thing: that Gallagher-ish delivery, all nasal protraction, is pretty hard to take in an un-"Wonderwalled" world and on "What Doesn't Kill You" he sounds like a newly humanoid cat, plaintive and struggling to shape its vowels ("you" becomes "yawowrhr"). There's an endearing, if slight love song in "Me and You" but the attempt at social commentary ("Messed Up Kids") is a lot less successful.'

The Independent was more accepting of what Bugg had done on his follow-up album, commenting, 'If the challenge faced by Jake Bugg on his second album is to prove you can take the boy out of Clifton without taking all traces of Clifton out of the boy, it's one he rises to. Those who see Bugg's so-called "authenticity" – whatever that means – as a storm of hype might spy signs of "grooming" in the decision to record in LA with producer Rick Rubin, but the follow-up to his hit debut makes the Midlands-to-Malibu move look largely seamless: as an exercise in expanded range, *Shangri La* is too diverse and distinct to dismiss.'

Tellingly, American reviewers were less concerned about issues of authenticity and accent than they were about the songs – maybe some were distracted by the freebie they got: some US radio stations received a gun-shaped bottle of tequila with 'What Doesn't Kill You' on the handle as well as the album. 'On Bugg's second album, Rick Rubin oversees an expanding sonic palette and a tougher sound; the punk-fired "What Doesn't Kill You" and grungy country rock of "All Your Reasons" push up against serenades like "Pine Trees", an alienated epistle that could've been cut in a winter cabin,' said *Rolling Stone* magazine.

USA Today said, 'On this follow-up to his swell debut, the 19-year-old Brit still rides the surprise that his nasal voice evokes. But the songs and presentation, aided by producer Rick Rubin, are evolving nicely too.'

'It would be easy for Bugg to slip into 1960s tribute-artist status, refusing to give up on peace and love,' said the *Washington Square News*. 'But instead of coming across as a cheap contemporary knock-off, Bugg emerges as a disciple –

someone who has studied these artists, knows what made them great and recreates their iconic sounds for a generation obsessed with synths and autotune. Bugg has created an album that can resonate across generations – suited for baby boomer throwbacks as well as millennial shout-outs. With *Shangri La*, Bugg proves he may be able to make a name for himself among the legends he admires. Rest assured, this is only the beginning.'

But what about the folks back home? What did those who helped Bugg get to where he was think of *Shangri La*? 'I think the album is strong,' is the response when I asked Dean Jackson of BBC Nottingham. 'Jake's debut was sure to be a difficult one to follow and the industry stock phrase "tricky second album" was sure to apply. But Jake seems to be making the transition from anecdotes about a lad growing up in Clifton to a young man with the world at his feet – with [the] trials and tribulations this brings – quite nicely, I love the gutsy tracks every much as bit as the more tender ones.'

NUSIC's Mark Del is typically bullish with his reaction to the album: 'Most 19-year-olds spend their summer jolly in Magaluf, and all they have to show for it is a new STD. Two weeks in LA and Jake crafted the foundations of a record that showed two fingers to second-album syndrome (sorry, couldn't resist). *Shangri La* manages to simultaneously stay consistent and evolve. With lyrics that reflect where Jake's come from, and where he's at now. Tracks for the acoustic lovers "Country Song" style, plus plenty of electric swagger for the Lightning Buggs. He's even written songs that last longer than a minute and fifty-three seconds. No, really.'

Mike Atkinson – whose article in *The Guardian* did so much to put Nottingham's musical profile on the national stage – reviewed the album for *LeftLion*: 'Like his sixties heroes, Jake Bugg prefers to bash his music out quickly. Recorded in a fortnight, *Shangri La* emerges just 13 months after his début, and there's a similar urgency to its opening volley of rattling, skiffley bangers. The scope widens as the album unfolds, but there are fewer all-acoustic moments, as the plaintive folkie of two years ago steps further into rockier territory. Dismissed by some as overly conservative, he's best viewed as a classicist, using vintage stylings to express present-day concerns. Some new influences emerge, ranging from "What Doesn't Kill You's" three-chord punk-thrash to the Neil Young flavourings of "All Your Reasons", but Jake's jaundiced view of his hometown is unchanged: "speed bump city" has become Slumville and "messed up kids" are still dealing blow on the corner. One day, he might yet pay tribute to our proud lace-making heritage and our vibrant creative business hubs – but you wouldn't want to bet on it.'

For the *Nottingham Post*, the album provided something of a dilemma: what if it was rubbish? What if the Clifton lad who could do no wrong... had gotten it wrong? 'Yes, that would be a difficult situation,' says entertainment editor Simon Wilson with a laugh. 'We'd probably just not mention how bad it was. In this case, it was a relief. I told him as much. If he'd have bombed it because he was so busy or not "feeling it" with Rubin or whatever, we'd have been in trouble because we write about him so much. It shifts between 1950s hillbilly to Neil Young rock to folk, garage and full-on country shuffles. As it turns out, *Shangri La* is as strong as the debut. If not more so. Ten of the twelve songs are earworms and obvious singles.'

As the album was waiting to be released, an extra bit of spice was added to the race to get it to Number One – if Jake managed it, *Shangri La* would be the 1000th Number One album in British chart history. Nearly 3,000 releases had made it to the top since 'Songs For Swingin' Lovers' hit the top spot for Frank Sinatra in July 1956.

But the competition would be tough – Robbie Williams and Eminem had releases pending at the same time and there was a One Direction album on its way too. If he did get to Number One when the album was released on 18 November, there was a good chance he'd be knocked off the following week by One Direction. 'I don't really see it like a competition,' Jake said. 'What I do and they do, it's for a totally different audience. It's not about that. But another Number One album would be nice though. Getting to Number One with my first album was a surprise; it'd be nice to add another to the collection.'

More symbolic in many ways, though, was an announcement made back home in Nottingham – Jake had booked a gig in the city for February 2014. It wasn't at Rock City… this time he would be playing the Nottingham Arena. Jake would be the first local act to headline the venue. 'Yeah, man, it's great,' he told the *Nottingham Post*. 'I never thought I'd be playing it. Obviously you dream of it but you don't actually think it will happen. I remember how many people were there for Kings Of Leon; it'll be crazy.'

The gig was scheduled to take place just a week before his 20th birthday – he'd still be a teenager when he headlined this massive gig. In a nice bit of nepotism that showed Jake still remembered his roots – and that it was important to *show* it too – it was announced that the support band at the Arena show would be The Swiines, the band that Jake was briefly a member of, fronted by his cousin Grant.

By way of contrast, Jake had another gig lined up in Nottingham too – and it promised to be a very different affair from a packed-out arena gig. It would be a show that would take him back to where it all started.

CHAPTER SIXTEEN

GO ON JB!

Soundtrack:
Bob Dylan – 'Lay Lady Lay' 1969
Nick Drake – 'Pink Moon' 1972
Paper Lace – 'Billy Don't Be A Hero' 1974

'It was amazing!' is the three-word review given to me by Gaz Peacham of Nottingham venue The Maze. He was describing Jake's gig that marked his return to the venue where it all started.

As Jake's autumn UK tour was in full swing, it was revealed that he planned to play four secret gigs along the way. Tickets were released via an online lottery – around a hundred tickets were released for each gig. He played the Old Queen's Head in London – the scene of his first ever gig in the capital – as well as King Tut's in Glasgow and The

Cavern in Liverpool, but it was his hometown return that was really generating interest.

The Saturday-afternoon show in Nottingham was held at the place where his live career started – one of the few places that would have him: The Maze. 'A lot of venues wouldn't let me play because I was 15,' he said backstage in an interview with the *Nottingham Post*. 'It's one of the reasons we chose The Maze for this show. We aren't doing Nottingham on this tour so I thought I'd do a little gig for anyone that wants to come along. It'll be good fun; an intimate show, letting people shout out what songs they want me to play.'

When he stepped out onto the tiny stage with just an acoustic guitar, there were football chants from opposing groups of Notts County and Forest fans, a bra was thrown and drinks were passed to Jake from the bar as the short set got underway. 'Go on JB!' one fan shouted as he rattled through songs from his debut album as well as tracks from his second, just days before its release. He also threw in a cover of 'Universal Soldier' for good measure. A 12 track online album of The Maze gig was later released on Spotify, giving fans a glimpse of what it would have been like to hear Jake play at The Maze in his early days... albeit with a much bigger and noisier audience. 'It was great to see Jake back on that stage and playing to a full room who sang every word back to him,' manager Gaz Peacham says. 'I think the last time Jake played here was probably maybe six months before he had his album go to Number One, so it was a very quick turnaround. It was also a huge thing to talk to Jake and hear him say how much he appreciated The

Maze for giving him gigs in his early days. It was also good to see that, even with all the non-stop attention he now gets, he is still really down to earth and a nice guy.'

It's said that nice guys finish first – but that wasn't to be the case when *Shangri La* was released a week after the gig at The Maze. All eyes were on Jake, with a real expectation that he could get his second Number One album in a row. But by midweek it looked like part-time Take That star Robbie Williams was just sneaking ahead with his *Swings Both Ways* album. The industry seemed to want Williams to succeed: 'It is fitting that Robbie Williams is in the lead to become the 1000th Official Number One Album,' said Martin Talbot, chief executive of the Official Charts Company. '*Swings Both Ways* echoes the very first Number One album, Frank Sinatra's *Songs For Swingin' Lovers*.'

As ever, Bugg did a chillingly accurate impression of someone who wasn't that arsed either way: 'It's not as important as the sales of the album,' he said. 'It'd be great for it to sell a million copies like the first one did but being at Number One doesn't really matter.'

In the end, *Shangri La* entered the UK charts at Number Three – Robbie Williams swung the top slot and Eminem was second. Some consolation was to be found in the fact that Bugg's album made it to the top of the Official Record Store Chart, which reflects sales from the UK's independent record shops. But a more telling statistic came a little later from America: *Shangri La* entered the US charts at Number 46... some 29 positions higher than his debut album did earlier in the year. *Billboard* magazine asked Jake for his formula for success: 'You just write some tunes and see what happens, see what comes up,' he said. 'You never know what's going to happen. That's the exciting bit of it. It's hard to say what's going to happen.' Bugg was booked in for a 19-date North American tour at the start of 2014 and commented, 'I'm just going to have to tour it and play my songs and see what happens really. That's all I can do is keep chipping away with it and see how people react.'

Typical Bugg: a moochy shrug, a not-bothered sideways look... and just get on with it. He appears to be as 'heroically un-arsed' offstage as he is on. Some find this aspect of Jake frustrating; in an age of trained, soundbite-savvy musicians who are always on their best game, Bugg stands out as someone who not only refuses to play the game, he's deliberately turned up without his kit. 'I like him because he is what he is,' says Simon Wilson of the *Nottingham Post*, who has tracked Jake's progress more than anyone. 'I quite like that he's just being himself – and in all the times I've interviewed him, he's been exactly the same – every single time. I must admit the last time I spoke to him, backstage at Splendour, he was slightly jollier than he is normally and actually smiled a few times and made a joke about some girl in Portugal who lifted her top up at a gig and was distracting him. She didn't realise she was on the big screen and all the rest of it. In a way, he represents working-class Nottingham a lot better than if he was jumping about and being all showbizzy. I really hope he doesn't get affected by everything that is going on because we like him like that. I don't think he will, as he's got some decent local people around him like Jason Hart.'

Gaz Peacham of The Maze, whose association with Jake stretches right back to the very start, agrees: 'I think he is a bit like that [moochy] but I think he's also quite shy. But I think he's hard working. Speaking to Jake, right from his early days – and I'm sure he's changed his opinions and he's a lot more worldly now – I think he's quite a sharp cookie. And I think he's very passionate, he's always been very passionate about music.'

Someone who's also been tracking Bugg from the early days is Zoe Kirk, who made the *This Is Live* video of Jake when he was barely 16. What's her take on what makes Bugg stand out? 'Something fresh, I guess, there is something a little bit different about him. He's not loud and obnoxious and he's not "try harder" in terms of promotion and PR. He's quite natural. When I met him, he was like a nice laid-back guy and his style is something different – he has that Bob Dylany kind of feel. There's quite a few folky singer songwriters but the tone of voice that he has and the Dylany style has set him apart from the other folk acts at the moment, I would say.'

The Bugg effect on the Nottingham music scene is undeniable. The city – and the way it's perceived musically – has changed because of Jake and his success. Gaz Peacham of The Maze again: 'I think it has changed Nottingham – we've never had an artist who's had the sort of success that Jake's had in the last couple of years. In a way, it's the biggest expectation ever. Nottingham has always had one of these scenes before where everyone was always saying, "There's loads of good acts in Nottingham, why aren't any of them blowing up and getting more success?" Now we've got Jake Bugg. Now it's changed to, "Who's the next Jake Bugg going to be? Who's the next one that's going to blow up?" And also because it was a solo act, just one guy, that makes it more interesting as well. Because if it had been a band, people would be saying, "Are they all from Nottingham? Did they just go to uni in Nottingham? Maybe they lived in Nottingham but were born in this place and that place." Whereas Jake is Nottingham through and through.'

Yet not everyone in the city completely understands Bugg and his success: 'I don't get why he's big to be honest,' says Nottingham Rock City DJ Ron Upton, continuing with refreshing honesty: 'There's not enough that's new or different about it to differentiate it from Liam Gallagher singing Bob Dylan songs. In my head, that's what it is. It works because there hasn't been anything like it for a while. It's from the current generation's dad's record collections. They can relate to it because they haven't heard it before. That kind of "fuck you" attitude. It's playing the same music with a different gesture – the notes and chord sequences but with a slightly different sneer. That's the beauty of it, it works.'

'If there's a legacy of what Jake's done so far it's that he's laid to rest the ghost of Paper Lace,' says Dick Stone, former programme director of Trent FM, where Jake appeared on one of the station's podcasts. 'So it's no longer, "Ah yes,

Nottingham – the only thing they've ever done is Paper Lace way back when. And nothing since."'

Nearly 50 years after they formed, Paper Lace are still gigging. So they must be doing something right. The band's name comes up in virtually every conversation about Nottingham music and Jake's success – so it seems reasonable to ask lead singer Phil Wright what he makes of Bugg and his music. 'I like his material,' he told me. 'I don't think he's particularly new but he's new to the generation that are around today. I like the stuff that he's doing, he's got a lot of attitude, I think it's quite melodic, but that's me – I'm a sucker for melody – and I think he's a great performer. He's so young, he could develop into something quite huge. I think he's a great guy, he's modest enough, it doesn't appear to have gone to his head. He seems to know what he wants, produces decent music, he's got a great voice. He's got, I believe, people clamouring to play with him and be associated with him. In the seventies, it was a different era, when anything went. Now I think, with the advent of a lot of singer songwriters since that point, you're getting serious music. There's more competition – but there's only eight notes out there! People have heard stuff over and over again and compare it with other stuff. So there's all that, along with carving yourself a career in music and I hope he's got the right people around him to guide him through it all because he's a young guy, I mean, crikey – the world at your feet at 20, amazing isn't it?'

I asked the ever affable Phil Wright if there wasn't just a

small part of him that was annoyed when Jake took Paper Lace's crown as The Last Nottingham Number One: 'The last Number One? No, I would never think like that. I am proud of the place I come from and the music it produces and, if it's worthwhile, I'm behind [it] a hundred per cent. Give Jake my undying support for ever. He's someone who's clambered through and stuck his head above the parapet – he's good enough to stay there long term.'

Nottingham's always been a musical city – the difference now is that people *outside* of Nottingham know it's a musical city. The potential danger here is that Jake Bugg is a one-off – the Paper Lace of his day. 'We need another Jake,' says Mark Del of *NUSIC*, who spends much of his time going into schools to talk to kids about the music industry. 'If it's only him, the scene becomes The Jake Bugg Story. Another artist needs to come through. I think that will be Indiana. Dog Is Dead are building it live. For me, Indiana can go Top Twenty and get a Mercury nomination. If another Jake comes through and everyone goes, "Oh, it's a Jake Bugg wannabe," and they go in at Number One because they write great songs and people love them… then it's a good problem to have. But I love the diversity so, in an ideal world, I'd love the next big Nottingham act to be from a significantly different genre to Jake. But if a great singer-songwriter came through who wrote great songs that connected with enough people to send him into the Top Ten of the album chart… Jake realising his dream in such a competitive area is almost as inspiring for an aspiring doctor, or boxer or business person, as it is for a musician. Because he's someone who has done what seems like the impossible. It's inspiring. And for some reason, it's more inspiring if that person lives near us. Even if you don't have a connection to Jake Bugg, the fact that you live in the same city as him can inspire you.'

'This is our purple patch,' says Nottingham's Mr Music George Akins, 'but is it a good enough purple patch? Probably not – Jake's one act. He went to Number One, brilliant, but there's so much more talent out there. Let's try and have a city that continually produces good music, continually has champions, continually has people that are going to expose it and have a spotlight on our city for A&Rs and other people looking for talent. We have a massive spectrum of styles – there's no clear Nottingham sound. Jake is different from Dog Is Dead, Dog Is Dead is different from Indiana, then you've got Georgie Rose, who's really exciting, who's a little bit more like Laura Marling; there's a twinge of Elvis Presley about her – she's fantastic. Then you've got other acts like Kagoule, grungier and a bit heavier, and Kappa Gamma are bit more in the stable of Dog Is Dead. Ady Suleiman and Rob Green are more R&B, then there's Harleighblu. Then we have this amazing soul singer called Natalie Duncan – she's a wonderful soul, jazz singer with a piano. And then after that we're looking for the next thing and we're continually looking for that. The Jake story is probably the greatest one and will anyone get as big as Jake? Hopefully someone will. Will Jake continue? I can't see why not, I can't see why he won't go on to be a career artist.'

NUSIC's Mark Del has his predictions for Nottingham's musical future too: 'There's a good ten odd Nottingham acts who could blow up in 2014, the Champions League places probably going to Indiana, Ady Suleiman, Amber and Saint Raymond. Each one has a Top Twenty album in them, I have no doubt. Casting our eye to the Europa League, Harleighblu and Kagoule are both acts I can see touring the world to rapt crowds, France is already falling in amour with Georgie Rose, Fearne Cotton seems to have a crush on Joel Baker and Ronika's debut album will be a cult classic exciting hipsters, producers and men who like men in equal measure. Man, I haven't even mentioned the two best live bands I've seen this year! Noah and Baby Godzilla. Well, I have now.'

Jake and the city of Nottingham are riding a wave – there's even talk of people exaggerating or even faking their Notts credentials as it's seen as the musical place to be. Jake's sound is of the past but it's relating to the now. And it's a sound that, ironically, is influencing the very type of music Bugg so clearly despises: 'I think that the sound that Jake has is along the same lines and in the same sphere as the likes of Ed Sheeran and that's the current wave,' says Dick Stone, who's now programme director of Capital FM in Nottingham. 'It's like the Britpop wave a good few years ago. They were all different but also very similar in some ways. I think Jake's the cutting edge of that. I don't think he's the pioneer of it – there were some people who made headway prior to Jake – but he was one of the first. And it went into the mainstream, rather than remaining as a niche.

That's exemplified when you watch the epitome of mainstream – something like *X Factor*. Look at the number of people who appear on *X Factor* who are singer-songwriters with a guitar. They would never have been there two or three years ago. Now when people do that, it doesn't look fresh or new. You think: Oh, it's a Jake Bugg clone.'

Jake's appropriation of 'old' music and making it relatable – or palatable – to a different audience is an issue that comes up time and time again. 'I just like a lot of the old stuff,' he says. 'That's not to say some of the contemporary stuff that's in the charts ain't good as well. If it's got a good tune, bang on. But a lot of it doesn't sound good to me.'

From a marketing and sales point of view though, it's the ideal situation: the oldies will like it because they can relate to it from their youth and the young 'uns like it because it speaks to them as something 'new'. Double bubble. Bugg himself has a perfectly simple answer to this: 'Any music we haven't heard yet is new music, no matter how old it is.'

But why him? Why now? Anyone walking into a betting shop three years ago and putting good money on the next big thing being a teenager from the East Midlands playing countryfied rockabilly folk with a council-estate twist – 'Bob Dylan with an ASBO', as writer and broadcaster Stuart Maconie put it – would have been shown the door. In some ways, no one is more surprised than Bugg himself about what's happened to him: 'When I was younger and writing my very first songs, obviously you dream of a life like this,' he told the *Liverpool Echo*. 'But I never once thought that it would actually happen, especially not to the level I've got to now. Honestly, I never thought it would pan out like this, or this quickly.'

Bugg's success, and the way his home city has dealt with it, is unusual. The way that success affects people can work against them. The other character in this story is the Clifton estate. Singing about escaping from it has given Jake Bugg the ability to do just that: escape. Bugg hasn't moved from Clifton as such – he's never there because he lives in hotels and airport lounges. There is a joke along the lines of: why is Liverpool airport named after John Lennon? Because it's the first place he headed to when he made any money. It's a predictable part of the trajectory of many musicians that, as soon as they reach a level where they get national recognition, they leave the town that got them there. But Jake and other musicians who are enjoying the groundswell of success that Nottingham is experiencing seem to be staying loyal to the city: 'They're not feeling they have to go to London anymore,' says Mark Del. 'Why? Because there's a scene here – they feel part of something and they want to stay part of it. Why would Jake now – well over a million albums in – suddenly move to London? He would have done it a year ago when it was all taking off. As I understand it, Jake is planning to stay in Nottingham. The thing that might change that is love... if he gets a long-term superstar girl-friend in London. I think Jake's planning to buy a house in Nottingham, I don't think it's in Clifton...'

When musicians break out of the city they come from, there's usually a backlash whereby their hometown tries to cut them down to size. One of the places that Bugg is rumoured to have been looking to buy a house is the posh Nottinghamshire town of Southwell; another tale is that he's now got a Mercedes with a BUGG number plate – both of which he's denied – and that maybe he will leave the area. But in Bugg's case – even though he's barely been there since his success kicked in – he and Nottingham are staying loyal to each other. Simon Wilson of the *Nottingham Post* says, 'Certainly from a media point of view, there's no, "Let's bring him down, let's expose him." He bought that $20,000 guitar in Nashville. I spoke to him last week, he was in a shop in London buying one for £22,500 – a Gibson gold top. And you think: Fucking hell – why shouldn't he? Because he's sold a million copies of his album, so what's he going to spend it on? He could be chucking it away on gambling, drugs and all sorts. He actually sees it as an investment anyway – the guitars aren't going to lose any value. There have been mutterings amongst a few musicians since he got successful. Not like, "Oh, he's really changed," or that nonsense, more like, "His album's not as good as one I could write," or something. But generally speaking, everyone's just loving it because it's brought attention to the city.'

But is Bugg loving it? There are signs he may be struggling with that gap between reality and expectation. There is no better example of how things have changed for him than the photos that were published in the press at the end of 2013. They showed Bugg posing with his guitar in a photo shoot for fashion house Saint Laurent: 'Nottingham-born musician Jake

Bugg has joined the ranks of music legends who have posed for Hedi Slimane's Saint Laurent Music Project,' wrote Bibby Sowray in the Fashion section of the *Telegraph*. 'The series of portraits continue the French fashion house's strong affiliation with the music world, which was started by founder Yves Saint Laurent when he dressed Mick and Bianca Jagger for the 1971 wedding in St Tropez. For his portrait Bugg wears his own Saint Laurent motorcycle jacket and was shot by Slimane in Malibu whilst recording his second album, *Shangri La*. Bugg and Slimane's friendship began when Slimane arrived at Saint Laurent as creative director in March 2012, at which point Bugg visited him in Paris. At the time Bugg was a fledgling star and had not yet released his self-titled debut album, which went to Number One in the UK charts.'

It really is a world away from that shell-suited kid with a guitar on his back, grabbing a bus from Clifton to the city centre to get a school-night gig. His success is considerable but he seems almost guilty about it. 'When I go back to Clifton, the general talking point with people most of the time is money,' he told *Q* magazine in December 2013. 'I don't like to talk about money but you see how people worry about it so much. Whereas me, I can now do what I wanna do and I feel terrible. I'm making up for the things I never had but I feel guilty every time I buy a new pair of trainers. It feels *wrong* somehow.'

Nottingham promoter George Akins believes Bugg has what it takes to make the most of what he's done so far, and even go further: 'He's a very down-to-earth guy, he's from a council estate, tasted some fame very young, but he dealt with it very well from what I see of him. He's hard working and he's talented.'

Few doubt Bugg's talent but some have questioned his use of other songwriters – it's been an easy stick to beat him with for those who enjoy that particular practice. It's left an aftertaste, though, of 'Bugg the puppet' – as much in thrall of older songwriters and managers as any of the acts peddling the kind of 'X *Factor* shit' he claims to hate so much: 'Jake is a big contradiction in many ways,' says BBC Nottingham's Dean Jackson. 'Some people think he is naïve, I don't think he is. I actually think he is incredibly intelligent. I think he's very level-headed and he gets what is going on around him. So any notion that he is a puppet or out of his depth is untrue. I think he's coping very well. I spoke to him on the phone, probably a fortnight, three weeks ago, and the conversation was as down to earth as ever. He's never boasted to me on one occasion, he's never sounded in awe of what's happening on any occasion and he's never implied in any way shape or form that he's moved on. It's a cliché, but to me, he's exactly the same person now as he was when he walked into our studio.'

But according to Bugg, the songwriting collaborations may be a thing of the past. Jake says he wants to shed the rockier songs – the kind of tunes that *Shangri La* was toploaded with – and return to his acoustic roots – something along the lines of sensitive British singer songwriter Nick Drake: 'I don't want to work with anyone else,' he told the *NME*. 'I want to make an acoustic record, something not necessarily with big choruses. For example, [Nick Drake's 1972 album] *Pink Moon* – you take one of those tracks separately, it doesn't stand up but, if you take it all together, it creates a mood, an atmosphere.'

The collaborations may have borne fruit but he now seems to view them as having been a necessity rather than something he pursued or wanted: 'That's kind of the way it works now because labels don't have a lot of money so they want to be sure they have the best chance they can at making some.'

But if you sell a million records and go from open-mic nights to Nottingham Arena in the space of three years, record labels are far more likely to listen to you... certainly more so than if you are a 15-year-old in a shell suit catching a bus to The Maze.

Bob Dylan was twenty before he released his first album – Jake Bugg, the young man whose name has appeared in the same sentence as Dylan's on so many occasions in recent years, has managed two by the age of nineteen. To some, he may well be The Council Estate Bob Dylan, The Cockiest Lonnie Donegan Wannabe in Nottingham, or The King of the Clifton Delta. These seem to be largely flags of convenience for journalists and commentators who don't quite know what to make of him or understand why the music of two generations ago has suddenly connected with kids who are supposed to have lost interest in rock.

But what does Bugg himself attribute his success to? Why him? Why now? His answer is typically short and to the point. It has, as ever, very few whistles and bells on it: 'I'm just a guy playing a few songs,' he says.

CHAPTER SEVENTEEN

A NOTTINGHAM GLOSSARY

The city of Nottingham and its surrounding areas have a language of their own. If you're going to walk the walk, you better be able to talk the talk. Here are some useful words that are peculiar to the area – don't even get me started on the accent. Thanks to Simon Wilson of the *Nottingham Post* with this section – I suggest you don't leave your aahse without it.

Aahse – abode, dwelling
Arse end – bottom
Beeroff – off-licence, place to buy alcohol
Bobbo – horse
Buttie – sandwich
Clout – smack

Cob – bread roll

Croggy – to give someone a lift on your bike

Duck – term of endearment, similar to 'love' or 'dear'

Feds – police officers

Frit – frightened

Gawping – staring

Kak handed – clumsy

Manky – scruffy or dirty

Mardarse – a softy, a cry baby

Mardy – sulky, not happy at all

Mash – to make a pot of tea

Mithering – bothering

Nesh – sensitive to the cold

Nowt – Nothing

Parky – cold

Peng – something really good

Physog – face

Rammel – rubbish

Sucker – lolly

Summat – something

Tabs – ears

Trap – mouth

Twitchell – a narrow passageway

Tuffees – sweets

Wappy – mental or crazy